4

Peter W. Becker

Recognition of Patterns

Using the Frequencies of Occurrence of Binary Words

Second, revised edition

Springer-Verlag
Wien New York

Dr. Peter W. Becker
Electronics Laboratory
Technical University of Denmark
Lyngby, Denmark

With 24 Figures

Library of Congress Cataloging in Publication Data

Becker, Peter W
    Recognition of patterns using the frequencies of
occurrence of binary words.

    Bibliography: p.
    1. Pattern perception. I. Title.
Q327.B4 1974   001.53!4   74-13582

ISBN 3-211-81267-9 Springer-Verlag Wien—New York
ISBN 0-387-81267-9 Springer-Verlag New York—Wien

TABLE OF CONTENTS

PREFACE

The work described in this publication was initiated at the General
Electric Company's Electronics Laboratory, Syracuse, N.Y., U.S.A. The
author would like to take this opportunity to express his gratitude to
the Electronics Laboratory for its support and encouragement in this work.
Thanks are in particular due to Mr. J.J. Suran for his continued interest
and help. It is impossible to acknowledge all the help the author has received from members of the Laboratory staff. However, the author is particularly indebted to Mr. T.C. Robbins for managing the building of the
word recognizer (described in Section 7.4) and for many helpful discussions.
Thanks are also due to Mr. W.E. Sollecito for valued support and direction,
and to S.M. Korzekwa, S.B. Akers, Jr., and B.L. Crew for many discussions
on implementation and design of pattern recognizers. Part of the work has
been sponsored by two departments of the General Electric Company, the
Large Jet Engine Department and the Apollo Support Department. The author
is grateful for the permission from the two departments to publish results
of theoretical interest in this dissertation.

The work was later continued in Denmark, supported by two grants: no.
1382 in 1966 and no. 1511 in 1967, received from the Danish Government
Fund for Industrial and Scientific Research. The author is grateful to
said Fund, and thereby the Danish taxpayers, who gave the author an opportunity for uninterrupted work with pattern recognition problems.

In August 1967 the author joined the staff of the Electronics Laboratory, Technical University of Denmark, where the subsequent pattern
recognition work took place; the author is happy to acknowledge his debt
to the members of the staff and to his students for many stimulating and
helpful discussions.

Most of all, however, the author would like to thank his wife,
Bodil, for wholehearted support during the work with this book.

P. W. B.

Electronics Laboratory

Technical University of Denmark

Lyngby

GLOSSARY OF SYMBOLS

A	A class of patterns, Section 2.2.
a	Sample mean frequency for members of Class A, Section 4.1.
B	A class of patterns, Section 2.2.
B(j)	The expected cost of classifying a C_j member with the minimaxing procedure; Subsection 1.6.3.
b	Sample mean frequency for members of Class B, Section 4.1.
C_i	Pattern class no. i of the N_C classes.
d	The distance between means of Class A and Class B, Subsection 6.4.3.
$E\{\cdot\}$	The symbol indicates the computation of the expected value of the quantity in brackets.
FOBW	Frequency of Occurrence of Binary Words, Subsection 1.1.1.
f	The frequency of occurrence of the binary word Ψ is called f_ψ, Section 2.2, Steps 4 and 5.
G_1	Average information about classmembership given by Ξ_1; Subsection 1.5.4, Paragraph (4).
IP	Index of Performance, Section 1.6.
J_{AB}	The symmetric divergence; Subsection 1.5.4, Paragraph (5).
K_{ij}	The cost of classifying a member of class no. i as being a member of class no. j, Subsection 1.4.1, Paragraph (b).

$(K_i)_k$ The average cost incurred when all patterns represented by points in W_k are classified as C_i members, Subsection 1.6.1.

L_k The likelihood ratio for micro-region W_k, Subsection 1.6.4.

M_A The centroid for Class A points, Subsection 6.2.4.

M_{AD} The number of Class A members in the design data group, Section 2.2, Step 3.

M_{AT} The number of Class A members in the test data group, Section 2.2, Step 3.

M_B The centroid for Class B points, Subsection 6.2.4.

M_{BD} The number of Class B members in the test data group, Section 2.2, Step 3.

M_{BT} The number of Class B members in the design data group, Section 2.2, Step 3.

MS   Measure of Separability, Subsection 1.5.4.

N_C Number of pattern classes.

N_H The largest number of attributes that can be implemented in the hardware (or software) realization of the pattern recognizer.

N_p The number of attributes from which the set of p attributes is selected, Subsection 1.5.6.

$P(x,y,z)$ A trivariate density from Equations 6.21 and 6.22, Subsection 6.4.7.

P_k The probability of a pattern point falling in W_k, Subsection 1.6.1.

$P(i)_k$ The probability of a point representing a C_i member falling in W_k, Subsection 1.6.1.

P_M Midpoint of $120°$ r-circle arc, Subsection 6.4.5.

$P_{pr}(i)$ — The a priori probability of the appearrance of a member of pattern class no. i, Subsection 1.4.1, Paragraph (a).

PR — Pattern Recognizer.

p — The number of attributes which is used, $\Xi_1, \ldots, \Xi_p$, $p \leq N_H$, Figure 1.1.

P_ψ — Binary word probability, Section 3.1.

q — The number of measurements, $T_1, \ldots, T_q$, Figure 1.1.

R^* — Bayes' risk; Subsection 1.6.2.

$R(j)$ — The expected cost of classifying a C_j member with Bayes' procedure, Subsection 1.6.2.

r — A correlation coefficient used in Subsections 5.3.5 and 6.4.2.

S — A measure of separability, Chapter 4.

S_H — The number of hyperplanes, Subsection 1.7.4.

s — A particular value of the standard deviation, Sections 6.2 and 6.4.

T — Thresholdsetting, Figures 1.2, 1.3, and 4.1.

v^2 — Sample variance, Section 4.1.

$v(t)$ — A waveform pattern, Subsection 5.4.3.

W_k — Micro-region no. k, Subsection 1.6.1.

X_i — The binits X_1, X_2, etc.; they are logic '0's or '1's, Chapter 3.·

Z — A stochastic process, $Z=Z(\Phi_1, \Phi_2, \ldots)$, Section 5.1.

α   Alpha. A ratio defined by Equation 6.10, Subsection 6.4.2.

β   Beta. A ratio defined by Equation 6.10, Subsection 6.4.2.

Γ   Gamma. Number of uncorrelated N-grams in a segment consisting of L binits, Section 3.1.

γ   Gamma. Number of Γ N-grams which are of the form Ψ, Section 3.1.

δ   Delta. A coefficient defined by Equation 6.5, Subsection 6.2.2.

Ξ   Xi. The vector with the p coordinates $(\Xi_1, \ldots, \Xi_i, \ldots, \Xi_p)$, Section 1.3.

Ξ_i Attribute no. i, Figure 1.1.

ξ_j Xi. Value of attribute Ξ for pattern no. j, Equation 4.2.

ρ   Rho. The correlation coefficient.

σ   Sigma. The standard deviation.

τ   Tau. Time delay, Subsection 5.3.2.

Τ   Upsilon. Result of test no. q, Figure 1.1.

Φ   Phi. The parameters of the process Z=Z $(\Phi_1, \Phi_2, \ldots)$, Section 5.1; also the name of a machine, Article 1.7.3.4.

Ψ   Psi. Binary word, Section 2.2.

ω   Omega. ω/π is a sampling frequency, Subsections 5.3.2 and 5.4.3.

1.   PROBLEMS IN THE DESIGN OF PATTERN RECOGNIZERS

1.1 Introduction

1.1.1 About this Book. In this book a new method for the design of
pattern recognizers, PRs, is presented. The heart of the method is a non-
exhaustive, iterative procedure by which new effective pattern attributes
can be generated from existing, less effective attributes. With this
method each pattern is first reduced to a binary sequence by a suitable
coding method. Each sequence is then described in a statistical sense
by the observed frequency of occurrence of certain selected binary words.
The categorization of the patterns is performed on the basis of such observed values. Any pattern attribute used with this method is the observed
frequency of occurrence of some specified binary word. The method is
therefore called: The Frequency of Occurrence of Binary Words Method, or
the FOBW method. The method should also be of value to related disciplines
where pattern recognition concepts are used, e.g., artificial intelligence
and robotology.

The book is organized as follows. In the remaining part of Chapter
1 some general problems in the design of PRs are discussed. In Chapter 2
is described how a PR may be designed using the FOBW method. Certain steps
which were taken in Chapter 2 are discussed in the following four chapters.
A number of important and readily available publications are listed in the

bibliography.

The whole field of pattern recognition is new, and no all-comprehending theory is at present available. Time and again during the design of a PR it becomes necessary for the designer to make educated guesses, as will be seen in the following. This fact may make the design of PRs less of an exact science, but the importance of "the good hunch" adds a certain challenge to the work in this new field. For the purpose of this book a class of patterns is defined as a set of objects which in some useful way can be treated alike. A number of assumptions have been made in the body of the report. To make it clear when a restrictive assumption is introduced, the word assume will be underlined in each case.

1.1.2 The Two Phases in the Existence of a PR. The existence of a PR may be divided into two phases: the design phase (also called the learning phase), and the recognition phase. In the recognition phase the machine performs the following operation: when presented with an unlabeled pattern, the machine decides to which of some previously specified classes of patterns the given pattern belongs. One of the pattern classes could by definition contain "patterns not belonging to any of the other classes". The recognition phase is the "useful phase" where the PR performs work by classifying patterns and thereby helps the user to make decisions under conditions of uncertainty. The PR acts as a (perfect or imperfect) "clairvoyant" who reduces the economic impact of uncertainty for the user. The value of the PR's "clairvoyance" may be computed (Howard 1967); it has a strong influence on the price of the PR and on the user's preference of one PR over another.

Before the PR can recognize patterns reliably, the PR must have been trained somehow to pay attention to the significant pattern attributes. This training is performed during the design phase. The work described in this book is concerned only with the design phase.

1.2 Three Areas of Application.

The applications of PRs fall essentially into three areas.

1.2.1 Certain Acts of Identification.

This is the area where the human specialists are getting scarce or where they may be lacking in speed, accuracy or low cost. Some examples from this area will now be mentioned; in each case PRs have been reported to be successful or to hold much promise. Reading of alpha-numeric characters which may be impact printed or handprinted (Freedman 1972; Harmon 1972); much effort has been applied in this area where commercial applications seem to be abundant. The automated reading of other kinds of characters, e.g., printed Chinese (FIJCPR 1973 "CR II") or Japanese (Sugiura and Higashiuwatoko 1968; Masuda 1972) characters, has also been given attention due to the increasing interest in machine translation. There is a growing need for medical mass-screening devices of the PR type (Patrick 1974; SIJCPR 1974 "BM"). Steps in this direction have already been taken with regard to the inspection of electrocardiograms (Caceres et al. 1970) and blood pressure waves (Cox et al. 1972); also chromosomes (Caspersen and Zech 1973), blood cells (Bacus and Gose 1972), and X-ray pictures (Chien and Fu 1974) have been machine classified successfully. Other examples of acts of identification are: detection of cloud patterns (Tomiyasu 1974), roads (Bajcsy and Tavakoli 1974), remote sensing of the earth's resources (Nagy 1972) from satellite altitudes, automatic decoding of handsent Morse code (Gold 1959), jet engine malfunction detection based on engine

vibrations (Page 1967), identification of spoken words (Clapper 1971)
and of speakers (David and Denes 1972), fingerprint identification
(Eleccion 1973), and the solving of jig-saw puzzles (Freeman and Garder
1964). Two examples of PRs that perform acts of identification will be
described in Chapter 7.

1.2.2 <u>Decisions Regarding Complex Situations.</u> There are a number of decision making problems having the following two properties. (1) The
number of possible alternative decisions is relatively small, meaning
that the number of pattern classes N_C is relatively small. (2) The input
on which the decision must be based, meaning the unlabeled pattern that
should be classified, is hard to evaluate; in other words, the designer
has real difficulties finding an effective set of pattern attributes.
Three problems where the input has the form of a matrix will illustrate
this type of problem: prediction of tomorrow's weather from today's
weather map (Widrow et al. 1963; Booth 1973), and the selection of a
best move with a given board position in checkers (Samuel 1963; Samuel
1967) or in chess (Newell et al. 1963; Newell and Simon 1965; Greenblatt
et al. 1967; Good 1968). A number of problems concerning business and
military decisions are of the same "best move" type.

1.2.3 <u>Imitation of Human Pattern Recognition.</u> There are a number of
pattern recognition problems that are solved by humans with the greatest
of ease and which so far have been largely impervious to solution by machine. Typical of such problems are the reading of handwritten material
(Harmon 1972) and the identification of a person from an ensemble of
persons based on his handwriting or appearance (Goldstein et al. 1971).
Such difficult pattern recognition problems are of interest not only for

commercial reasons but also because their solution may shed light on cognitive processes. (Feigenbaum and Feldman 1963, Part 2; Deutsch 1967; Clapper 1971; David and Denes 1972).

1.3 The Configuration of a PR.

Before the design of a PR is discussed the structure of the finished product will be described briefly. Following the usual system description (Marill and Green 1960), a pattern recognizer consists of two parts, a receptor and a categorizer, as shown in Figure 1.1; preliminary processing is of no importance at this point, it will be discussed in Subsection 1.5.1. The receptor may also be referred to as the feature extractor or the characteristic calculator. The categorizer is also called the decision maker or the classifier. The functions of the two parts become apparent when it is considered how a PR (in the recognition phase) decides to which of several classes of patterns an unlabeled pattern belongs. The number of pattern classes is called N_c. In the receptor, the unlabeled pattern is exposed to a battery of different tests. The test results constitute a set of numbers T_1, T_2, ..., T_q, these numbers are processed in some manner to yield the set of numbers Ξ_1, Ξ_2, ..., Ξ_p that constitues the input to the categorizer. The p numbers may be illustrated geometrically by a point, called a pattern point, in a p-dimensional space, referred to as pattern space or decision space; the pattern point is called $\Xi = (\Xi_1, ..., \Xi_p)$. The p numbers are the values of the p attributes in terms of which the unlabeled pattern is now described. The concept "attributes" has also been known in the literature under the names: properties, features, measurements, characteristics, observables, and descriptors. The word "attributes" is used in this report because the other words have

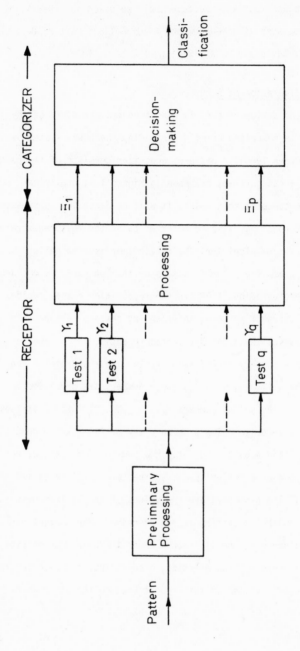

FIGURE 1.1 Block Diagram of a Pattern Recognizer.

wider uses; confusion seems less likely when the word "attribute" rather than one of the other words is selected to describe the attribute concept. The _categorizer_ stores information describing the rule according to which decisions are made. In this report the rule is _assumed_ to be non-randomized, meaning that the categorizer always makes the same decisions if the same pattern point $\Xi = (\Xi_1, \ldots, \Xi_p)$ is being categorized several times. The rule is equivalent to a decision function illustrated by a decision surface (also called separation surface) which partitions the p-dimensional space. The decision surface may be _implicitly_ defined as in the case of "Pandemonium" (Selfridge 1959). With this machine the N_c a posteriori probabilities of class memberships are computed given the location of the pattern point after which the pattern is classified as belonging to the most probable class. The decision surface may also be _explicitly_ defined as a geometric surface, e.g., parts of three hyperplanes may constitute a decision surface as will be illustrated by an example in Figure 1.6. The decision surface which is stored in the categorizer partitions the pattern space into N_c or more compartments. During categorization it is decided to which of the N_c pattern classes the unlabeled pattern belongs by:

(1) finding the compartment in which the pattern point corresponding to the unlabeled pattern is located; the compartments are so located that points in the same compartment as nearly as possible represent members of the same class of patterns.

(2) announcing the name of the pattern class which pattern points prevail in the compartment; this could be done by lighting a particular indicator light. There is usually no indication of the level of confidence associated with the decision.

The design of a PR is tantamount to a choice of tests, processing methods, and partitioning of the decision space. Notice that a PR always arrives at a decision based on the q measurements. Most of the PRs discussed in the literature perform all q tests on the unlabeled pattern. In cases where the tests are expensive the tests are performed one at a time and each new test is selected in the light of the results of the previously performed tests (much in the same manner the members of a panel show select new questions); machines where such deferred-decision or sequential-detection techniques are used have been described in the literature (Selin 1965, Chapter 9; Nelson and Levy 1968; Fu 1968; Mendel and Fu 1970, Chapter 2).

The designer's choice of tests, processing methods, and location of the decision surface is almost always influenced by constraints on time and funding, the weight and volume of the final implementation, etc. To appreciate how a designer may use the available techniques, it is instructive to summarize the factors that influence the design; this will be done in Section 1.4. Later, in Figure 2.1, a block diagram will be used to illustrate the procedure employed when a PR is designed by the "Frequency of Occurrence of Binary Words" method. A PR does not necessarily have to have the physical appearance of a special purpose computer; it could very well take the form of a program for a general purpose computer.

The problem of designing pattern recognizers may also be considered as a problem in mathematical linguistics (Fu 1974); this interesting approach is presently in the state of development and will not be discussed further. The basic idea is that any pattern can be reduced to a finite string of symbols and that classification (or labeling) of such strings is similar to mechanical translation of natural languages.

1.4 Factors that Influence the Design of a PR.

1.4.1 Factors Associated with the Pattern Classes. In the following

Class no.i ., i=1, 2, ..., N_C, is referred to as C_i. With each class of
patterns is associated a number of significant constants, the values of
which may or may not be known to the designer. The constants are related
to the following questions that may be asked about each class of patterns.
(a) What is the a priori probability, $P_{pr}(i)$, of an unlabeled pattern
being a member of C_i, rather than being a member of one of the (N_C-1)
other pattern classes? It may usually be assumed as will be done in the
following that the patterns will arrive according to some time-stationary
first order probability, and that they are not "maliciously" arranged in
any manner. The assumption is not always satisfied. Sometimes the class
memberships of arriving patterns show a Markov-dependence (Ma 1974).
At other times as in the case of letters in a text there are strong statistical relationships between adjacent letters (Thomas and Kassler 1967).
(b) What is the cost, K_{ij}, of classifying a member of C_i as being a
member of C_j? In the following it is assumed that K_{ij} does not change
with the percentage of misclassified members of C_i; utility theoretical
concepts are not applied. The convention will be used that K_{ij}, i≠j, is
non-negative and K_{ij}, is non-positive.
(c) Do the patterns change with time? If so, the parameter values used
in the PR must be adjustable and the values must be updated regularly
(Patrick 1972, Section 3.2.5). Unless otherwise indicated it is assumed
in the following that all distributions of pattern attribute-values are
stationary in time.
(d) How are the members of the same class related to each other, what is

the nature of the relationship? Do the members of each class consist of a typical pattern, a prototype, corrupted by noise? Or are the members of each class rather a collection of well defined, noisefree patterns, which have certain features in common (e.g., perfectly noisefree letters may be drawn in a great many ways (Akers and Rutter 1964))? Or do the class members have certain features in common while they at the same time all are somewhat corrupted by noise? Throughout this book it is assumed that the situation is basically probabilistic so that members of each class have certain features in common while they at the same time all are somewhat corrupted by noise.

(e) Is there reason to believe that C_i consists of several distinct subclasses, $C_{i,1}$, $C_{i,2}$, etc.? If so, the multivariate distribution of attribute values for members of C_i may very well be multimodal (meaning that the density of C_i-pattern-points has several local maxima in p-dimensional pattern space) or even disjointed (meaning that any path which connects two local maxima in pattern space must have at least one segment of finite length in a region where the density of C_i-points is zero). Multimodal, multivariate distributions can create difficult problems in the later categorization procedure as will be discussed in Article 1.7.2.2.

(f) Are the members of each class known to the designer through some "representative" members of the class? In such cases it is of greatest importance to ascertain that the sample members were representative when recorded, and that the processing in the data collection phase was performed with care so that the members remained representative. In the following it will be assumed that patterns which are taken to be representative of members of C_i are indeed representative of C_i members; with certain kinds of patterns (e.g. medical records such as ECGs) labeling (or classification) of the patterns cannot be done with 100% accuracy. In the case where the designer only has a representative collection of unlabeled patterns, he can attack the design problem by one of the methods described in the literature (Patrick 1972, Chapter 5; Duda and Hart 1973, Chapter 6).

Sometimes the designer uses data which previously have been used by other researchers for similar projects. In such cases the designer is able to directly compare the performance of his PR with the performance of the previously constructed machines. Presently the IEEE Computer society's Technical Committee on Pattern Recognition is compiling a readily available, well documented body of data for designing and evaluating recognition systems; data bases are available for impact- and hand-printed alphanumeric characters and for speech data.

1.4.2 Estimation of a PR's Performance. It may be instructive first to consider the following two special cases: use of "no attributes" and use of a set of "arbitrary attributes". No attributes is the limiting case where the designer simply does not design a receptor. In this case the designer uses only a priori information in the categorizer. A reasonable procedure is to classify all patterns as belonging to the class C_i for which the average cost of classification A_j,

$$A_j = (\sum_{\substack{i=1 \\ i \neq j}}^{N_C} P_{pr}(i) \cdot K_{ij}) + P_{pr}(j) \cdot K_{jj}$$

is minimized. The figure $(A_j)_{Min}$ is of importance to potential users when the justifiable cost of a PR with a specified performance is determined. If the designer selects a set of N_H attributes without regard for their effectiveness (and thereby saves some design effort) he has obtained a set

<u>of arbitrary attributes</u>. The mean accuracy which can be obtained with a PR using arbitrary attributes has been studied and was found to be discouraging (Duda and Hart 1973, Art. 3.8.4). The designer is almost always well advised to spend a large part of his design effort in selecting an effective set of attributes; the problem of finding an effective set of attributes will be discussed in Subsections 1.5.2 and 1.5.3.

In the remaining part of this subsection the usual case is considered where the designer generates N_p, $N_p \geq p$, attributes each of which there is reason to believe will be effective; from this set of attributes the designer selects a particular effective subset of p attributes by a suitable procedure such as the ones described in Subsection 1.5.6 and Section 2.5.

Before the recognition phase begins it is necessary to estimate how well the designed PR will recognize patterns. The popular procedure for obtaining such an estimate consists of first designing the PR using representative patterns, the so called design data, and then evaluating the PR by letting it separate a second set of representative patterns, the test data. The result of the separation of the test data is then considered an estimate of the PR's separating capability. Four design factors are associated with the estimate.

(a) The ratio between the number of patterns used for design and the number used for test. The question of how best to divide the available data has been discussed in Highleyman 1962a.

(b) The confidence intervals associated with the estimate. This matter has also been discussed (Highleyman 1962a;Duda and Hart 1973,Section 3.9).

(c) The minimum requirement for separation of the design data. After each preliminary design of a PR it is determined how many errors are made when the design data are separated. The question is then asked: have the design data by now been so well separated that it can be justified, timewise and budgetwise, to test the PR design with the test data to see if the PR design can meet the customer's specifications? Or is the separation of the design data so far from the goal that it would be wiser to look for a more effective subset of p attributes and redesign the PR before it is evaluated with the test data? Here, it should be recalled that although the design data and the test data both are samples drawn from the same set of N_c populations some differences must be expected between the two sample distributions. The PR design is optimized for the design data, the design can consequently be expected to give a poorer separation of the test data than of the design data. The question posed above does not seem to have been discussed in the literature. Usually, the PR design is evaluated with the test data as soon as the separation of the design data is somewhat better than the separation specified for the test data.

(d) Redesign of the PR using both design and test data for design. Assume that the designed PR is capable of separating the test data to satisfaction; let this PR be called PR1. Next let it be assumed that a new PR is designed using identical techniques and a set of design data that is the sum of the previous set of design data, DD1, and the previous set of test data TD1; let this PR be called PR2. If a new set of representative patterns, Test Data 2 or TD2, is introduced, will PR1 or PR2 separate TD2 more correctly? Recalling that DD1, TD1, and TD2 are sets of representative patterns from a population of patterns, it is obvious that due to the statistical fluctuations PR1 can on occasion separate TD2 better than PR2. In most cases it is, however, believed that PR2 will give better separation of TD2 than PR1. When time and funding permits, PR2 should be designed. The relative performance of PR1 and PR2 is a statistical quantity; it seems to have received no attention in the literature.

1.4.3 Four Major Problem Areas. In the remaining part of this chapter, the four major problem areas in the design of PRs are briefly reviewed. The problem areas are listed below.

(a) The selection of an effective set of attributes for the description of the patterns in question. This is the problem of what to measure.

(b) The selection of a decision procedure. This is the problem of how to categorize the receptor output, Figure 1.1.

(c) When the decision procedure has been selected there is usually a set of parameters to be evaluated. Here the problem is encountered of how to optimize the parameter values with respect to given representative patterns from the N_C different pattern classes.

(d) The realization in hardware of the receptor and the categorizer. Here the problem is raised of selecting forms of receptors and categorizers which will perform reliably when implemented, and which will meet the constraints on weight, volume, etc.

1.5 The Selection of the Attributes.

This section is organized as follows. First the preliminary processing of patterns and the generation of attributes is discussed. In Subsection 1.5.3 the important concept of an "effective set of attributes" is defined. Next some one-number-statistics are reviewed which may be used to measure how good one attribute is when used alone. After this, in Subsection 1.5.5 an important set of attributes, the templets of N_C prototypes, is described. The necessary concepts have now been developed to discuss ways of selecting an effective set of p attributes, this is being done in Subsection 1.5.6.

1.5.1 Preliminary Processing. The main operation in the receptor, Figure 1.1, is the computation of p attribute values, Ξ_1, Ξ_2, ..., Ξ_p, for the unlabeled pattern. Before the q measurements, T_1, ..., T_q, can be performed it often happens that the pattern must be isolated because other patterns and the background tend to obscure the pattern in question, e.g., letters in handwritten text or objects in reconnaissance photographs. Next the pattern may be exposed to preliminary processing where the designer takes advantage of his a priori knowledge of the recognition problem. E.G., (i) suitable filtering may be used to enhance the signal-to noise ratio for waveforms, (ii) handprinted alpha-numerical characters may be normalized with respect to size and orientation, (iii) irregularities that clearly are due to noise may be removed from the unlabeled pattern by "smoothing" so that edges become clearer (Duda and Hart 1973, Section 7.4) and (iv) the dynamic range for speech signals may be reduced (Hellwarth and Jones 1968).

One kind of preliminary processing is of particular importance in connection with the FOBW method: infinite clipping of waveform patterns. A waveform $v=f(t)$ is said to be infinitely clipped when only the sign of the amplitude, signum$\{f(t)\}$ = sgn$\{f(t)\}$, is retained and the magnitude, $|f(t)|$, is discarded. After infinite clipping the waveform has been reduced to a record of the zero crossing times. Infinite clipping may seem to cause a great loss of information. This impression is, however, not always correct. E.g., it has been conjectured, (Good 1967) that no loss of information whatsoever is suffered when a white noise signal is infinitely clipped as long as the signal is band-limited to the range (W_1, W_2) and $W_2/W_1 \leq (7+\sqrt{33})/4 = 3.186$. Even when some information is lost, it is not necessarily the information of interest to the designer. E.g., it has been found that the intelligibility of a clipped speech signal remains high although the quality of the reproduced sound has become poor (Lick-lider 1950; Fawe 1966; Scarr 1968). If the infinitely clipped waveform is sampled at a sufficiently high rate, almost all zero crossings will take place between two samples of opposite signs; each change in the string of sample signs will therefore indicate the location of a zero crossing with a margin of $\pm\frac{1}{2}$ of a sampling interval. The problem of how to recover information from infinitely clipped and sampled waveforms will be discussed further in Chapter 5.

1.5.2 Generation of Sets of Attributes in Practice. The designer can obtain some guidance in his search for a set of effective attributes by consulting with experts in the area of interest, by studying the litera-ture and by inspecting typical patterns. The possibilities are, however, often limited not only by restrictions on the PR with regard to size, weight, cost and processing time per pattern but also by constraints par-ticular for the problem at hand; two typical constraints will now be men-tioned. (i) The designer may be restricted to attributes, the values of which he can measure without storing the complete pattern (Bonner 1966); the frequencies of occurrence of specified short binary words in long binary sequences is an example of such attributes. (ii) In many pattern recognition problems the designer must look for attributes that show in-variance under the commonly encountered forms of distortion; e.g., in-variant attributes can be generated by moments (Hu 1962), integral geo-

metry (Duda and Hart 1973, Art. 9.3.7), diffraction-pattern sampling
(Lendaris and Stanley 1970) and by application of group theory (Grenander
1969; Watanabe 1972, pp. 453-478).

Often the patterns can be expanded using a set of orthonormal functions; in such cases the coefficients to the p most important terms of
the expansion may be used as attributes. The designer will select a set
of p orthonormal functions which is simple to store in the receptor and
which converges rapidly to the type of patterns in question; some of the
possibilities are: (i) "The fast Fourier transform" (Cochran et al. 1967)
which makes use of the Cooley-Tuckey algorithm, (ii) the Rademacher-
Walsh functions (Blachman 1974), Haar functions (Bremermann 1968, Section
VIII) and related expansions for functions of binary variables (Ito
1968), (iii) the Karhunen-Loeve expansion (Duda and Hart 1973, Section
6.14), and (iv) Wiener's Hermite-Laguerre expansion (Brick 1968).

To generate an effective set of p attributes two things are usually
needed: the p attributes should be selected as a best (or at least relatively good) subset from a larger set of attributes and some evolutionary
procedure (as for instance the FOBW method) should exist for improving
the subset of p attributes. The selection of the attributes is probably
the single most important step in the PR design; a witty description of
the search for good attributes and some of the pitfalls has been given by
Selfridge (Selfridge 1962).

1.5.3 An Effective Set of Attributes. The problem in receptor design is
to find an effective set of N_H or fewer attributes, where N_H is the largest
number of attributes which the designer can afford to use in the later
hardware (or software) implementation; p in Figure 1.1 is the number of

attributes that is actually used, p is usually equal to N_H. In rare cases when fewer than N_H attributes give adequate performance, p is less than N_H. The material in this subsection is divided as follows. First the concept of "an effective set of p attributes" is defined in Article 1.5.3.1. This definition leads to a definition of "the incremental effectiveness of an attribute Ξ_{p+1}" presented in Article 1.5.3.2.

1.5.3.1 A Definition of "An Effective Set of Attributes". The following definition is based on a discussion of "effectiveness of receptors", which has appeared in the literature (Duda and Hart 1973, Figure 1.1). Let it be assumed that the following are available to the designer.

(1) Two sets of p attributes S_1 and S_2 which may have several attributes in common; this is in principle equivalent to having two receptors R1 and R2 specified.

(2) A number of representative patterns that are divided into a Design Data group and Test Data group.

(3) A means for categorization. It could be a certain computer program for design of categorizers which are optimum in some sense, e.g., the number of misclassified patterns may be minimized by a computed linear separation surface. One such computer program will be described in Section 2.5. Other means for categorization and the problem of designing categorizers will be discussed in Section 1.7.

(4) An index of performance, IP, by which the performance of a PR can be evaluated; the convention will be used that higher values of IP illustrate better (rather than poorer) performance. The IP is largely determined by the decision procedure the designer uses (decision procedures will be discussed in Section 1.6). An example of an IP is "minus one times the

average cost per classification of a test data pattern"; this IP will be used by the designer in case he uses Bayes' decision. Notice that the designer in some practical cases may have to use a means for categorization that optimizes a feature (e.g., least number of misclassified patterns) that does not necessarily coincide with the IP (e.g., the average cost of classification, when $K_{ij} \neq K_{ji}$).

The designer now takes the following steps. (A) With the design data and R1 he computes the optimum categorizer, C1. He separates the test data using the PR consisting of R1 followed by C1. He computes the value of the index of performance for the test data, the value is called IP(1). (B) With the same design data and R2 he computes the optimum categorizer C2. He separates the test data using the PR consisting of R2 followed by C2. He computes the value, IP(2), of the index of performance for the test data. If IP(1) exceeds IP(2), the attribute set S_1 is said to be a more effective set of p attributes than S_2. Usually the performance of the PR has been specified in advance meaning that the index should have at least a certain specified value IPS. If IP(1) is close to or exceeds IPS, S_1 is said to be an effective set of p attributes.

The concept of effectiveness is conditioned on the available means for categorization and (what is usually less important) on the index of performance. If a set of p attributes is to be effective, it is necessary (1) that the members of each class tend to cluster at certain locations in the p-dimensional space, and (2) that no two clusters from the N_C sets of clusters coincide. What is less obvious but also important especially for large p-values is that (3) each of the N_C probability densities be essentially unimodal or at least not essentially disjointed so that N_C populations can be well separated by p-dimensional surfaces of simple form. When the last mentioned condition has not been met, it is doubtful whether the means for categorization will be capable of performing a satisfactory separation. This matter will be discussed further in Article 1.7.2.2.

1.5.3.2 A Definition of "The Incremental Effectiveness of an Attribute". Consider the case where the designer has (i) a set of p attributes, S_p, (ii) a set of (p+1) attributes, S_{p+1}, obtained by adding the attribute Ξ_{p+1} to S_p, (iii) a means for categorization, and (iv) an index of performance, IP. The designer can now compute the two values of the index, IP(p) and IP(p+1), in the manner described earlier. The PR designed with (p+1) attributes will always perform at least as well as the one designed with p attributes. The quantity IP(p+1)-IP(p) is called the incremental effectiveness of Ξ_{p+1}. The incremental effectiveness is conditioned on S_p, IP and the means for categorization.

1.5.4 One Attribute. The attribute is called Ξ_1, as in Figure 1.1. In this subsection it is discussed how the designer may estimate the effectiveness of Ξ_1. It is assumed that the probability density functions of the Ξ_1-values for members of Class 1, members of Class 2, etc., have been obtained; in practice normalized histograms are often used as approximations to the N_C probability density functions. It should be noticed that a set of p attributes each of which can take a finite number of discrete values, v_i, i=1, ..., p, in a sense may be considered as one attribute with a number of discrete values equal to the product: $v_1 \cdot v_2 \cdot \ldots \cdot v_p$. E.g., if Ξ_1 can take the values 2, 3 or 4, and Ξ_2 can take the values -1 and -5 then the "compound attribute"(Ξ_1, Ξ_2) can take the six discrete

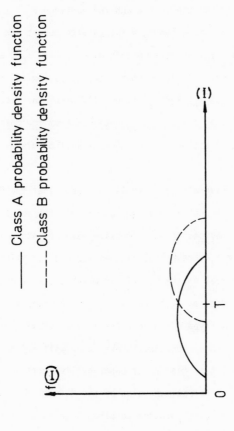

——— Class A probability density function

– – – – Class B probability density function

The members of Class A and Class B both with unimodal density functions may be separated by use of one threshold, T.

Figure 1.2

values (2,-1), (2,-5), (3,-1), (3,-5), (4,-1), and (4,-5).

The following notation will be used frequently in the remaining part of this report. The probability density function for members of Class A is called $f_A = f_A(\Xi_1)$; f_A has the mean a and the variance σ_A . The members of Class B have the density function $f_B = f_B(\Xi_1)$ with mean b and variance σ_B . The functions f_A and f_B, and the moments a, b σ_A^2 and σ_B^2, are usual-ly unknown to the designer. When it is stated in the following that the designer uses f_A, f_B, a, b, σ_A, and σ_B, it usually means that <u>the designer uses estimates of f_A, f_B, a, b, σ_A, and σ_B obtained from the normalized histograms.</u> The problem of estimating the moments will be discussed further in Section 4.1.

When Ξ_1 is an effective attribute it will be seen that the N_C density functions overlap little or not at all. No matter what the functional form of a separation surface may be, in one dimension categorization is achieved by establishing suitable Ξ_1-thresholds; Figures 1.2 and 1.3 illustrate two such cases. The interval on the Ξ_1-axis in which the Ξ_1-value of an unlabeled pattern falls decides the class to which the unlabeled pattern is assumed to belong. This type of categorizer is very simple to realize in hardware. When the designer sets the threshold he will try to optimize some measure of separability; "measure of separability" will in the follow-ing be abbreviated as MS. The optimum value of the MS will then give an estimate of how effective Ξ_1 is compared to other attributes. Three possible MSs will now be listed.

(1) The average cost of classifying a pattern, Bayes' criterion (Duda and Hart 1973, Chapter 2). This MS will be discussed further in Subsec-tion 1.6.2.

(2) The minimaxed average cost of classifying a pattern. The case $N_C = 2$

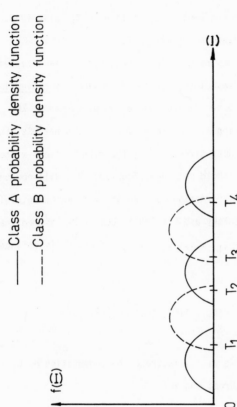

Figure 1.3

The members of Class A that have a trimodal, disjointed density function may be separated from the members of Class B that have a bimodal, disjointed density function by use of four thresholds, T_1, T_2, T_3, and T_4.

has been discussed in the literature (Selin 1965, Chapter 2). The case $N_C > 2$ will be discussed briefly in Subsection 1.6.3.

(3) Minimized error of the first kind for fixed value of error of the second kind, the Neyman-Pearson criterion; the MS can be used only when $N_C = 2$ (Davenport and Root 1958, Section 14-3; Selin 1965, Chapter 2), it will be discussed in Subsection 1.6.5.

These three MSs require that the designer has selected an optimum setting of the threshold(s); in the following the convention will be used that such MSs also are called indices of performance, IPs. IPs will be discussed in Section 1.6. There are, however, other MSs, the values of which may be computed directly from the distributions without a specification of the threshold settings. Four such MSs will now be listed.

(4) The average information, G_1, about class membership given by Ξ_1 (Lewis 1962; Kamentsky and Liu 1964). Let it be assumed that Ξ_1 can take v discrete values $\xi_1, \ldots, \xi_\ell, \ldots, \xi_v$, if so, G_1 is defined as follows (Lewis 1962).

$$G_1 = \sum_{i=1}^{N_C} \sum_{\ell=1}^{v} P(C_i, \xi_\ell) \log_2 \left(P(\xi_\ell | C_i) / P(\xi_\ell) \right)$$

A numerical example will illustrate the computation of G_1. Let N_C equal two and v equal three; and let

$P(C_1, \xi_1) = .31,$ $P(C_1, \xi_2) = .16,$ $P(C_1, \xi_3) = .03$

$P(C_2, \xi_1) = .01,$ $P(C_2, \xi_2) = .17,$ $P(C_2, \xi_3) = .32$

G_1 then becomes the sum of the $2 \cdot 3$ terms:

.31 $\log_2((.31/.50)/.32)+.16 \log_2((.16/.50)/.33)+.03 \log_2((.03/.50)/.35)+$

.01 $\log_2((.01/.50)/.32)+.17 \log_2((.17/.50)/.33)+.32 \log_2((.32/.50)/.35)$

$$G_1 \approx .52 \text{ bits}$$

(5) The symmetric divergence (Kullback 1959, page 6); this MS is applicable only in the case $N_C = 2$. With equal a priori probabilities the symmetric divergence J_{AB} is defined by the following expression.

$$J_{AB} = \int_{-\infty}^{\infty} (f_A(\Xi_1) - f_B(\Xi_1)) \ln(f_A(\Xi_1)/f_B(\Xi_1)) \, d\Xi_1$$

In the case with the six discrete probabilities listed above J_{AB} becomes the sum of three terms:

$(.62-.02) \ln(.62/.02)+(.32-.34) \ln(.32/.34)+(.06-.64) \ln(.06/.64)$

$$J_{AB} \approx 3.4$$

(6) The Fisher measure $(a-b)^2/(\sigma_A^2 + \sigma_B^2)$; this MS was proposed by R.A. Fisher (Fisher 1963; Duda and Hart 1973, Section 4.10). The MS is applicable only in the case $N_C = 2$.

(7) The measure of separability S which is proposed in Chapter 4 of this book.

$$S = |a-b|/(\sigma_A + \sigma_B)$$

This MS is applicable only in the case $N_C = 2$.

The designer must decide which of the seven MSs is most meaningful

in his case; maybe he would prefer some other MS, the possibilities are
by no means exhausted. When the designer has made his choice he can estimate the effectiveness of all the attributes of interest.

It will be shown in Subsection 1.7.4 that the problem of separating
N_C pattern classes may be reduced to a set of problems of separating two
classes. The constraint $N_C = 2$ is consequently not very restrictive in
practice.

1.5.5 Templet Matching. Whenever the members of a class all consist of
a class prototype plus some corrupting noise it is reasonable to use the
agreements with templets of the N_C prototypes as attributes. The match
between an unlabeled pattern and each of the templets is determined in the
receptor. Next it is decided in the categorizer if the unlabeled pattern
agrees well with one and only one of the templets. If so, the pattern is
regarded as belonging to the corresponding pattern class; otherwise the
pattern is rejected. The reading of printed or typed characters is typical
of cases where templet matching can be applied with little or no preliminary processing of the raw data. In other cases the templet is applied to
a pattern obtained from the unlabeled pattern by a suitable transformation
with some normalizing properties; e.g., the transformation of the unlabeled pattern could make use of integral geometry (Duda and Hart 1973, Art.
9.3.7) or the auto correlation function (Horwitz and Shelton 1961).
A common problem with two-dimensional patterns is to obtain a templet
which is invariant to (i) vertical and horizontal shifting, and (ii) rotation and magnification. One possible way of solving the problem is to
(a) generate the two-dimensional auto-correlation function (it is invariant

to the shifting), (b) plot the polar-coordinates of the auto-correlation function in a carthesian coordinate system so that x equals the logarithm of the radius vector and y the vectorial angle, (c) find the two-dimensional auto-correlation function for the figure in the carthesian system, it will be invariant to shifts in the vectorial angle and to shifts in the logarithm of the radius vector; in other words the templet is invariant to shifting, rotation and magnification.

To use the templet matching technique it is necessary to introduce some measure of the match between the unlabeled pattern and each of the N_c templets; one possible measure is the crosscorrelation between the pattern and the templets (Duda and Hart 1973, Sec. 8.3.).

If it is known that only one templet will match the unlabeled pattern the search can be stopped when such a templet has been found. On the average $N_c/2$ templets must be checked before the pattern is identified. When an exhaustive search through all N_c templets is not required, two things can be done to accelerate the recognition procedure. (1) If the patterns appear in certain contexts (which is contrary to the assumption in Paragraph (a) in Subsection 1.4.1) the templets may be searched in such a manner that the most likely class memberships (judging from the last few recognized patterns) are checked first. This situation is for instance encountered when the patterns are letters in an ordinary English text (Thomas and Kassler 1967). (2) If the number of classes is large, the classes may be divided into a smaller number of super-classes, for each of which a templet is developed. As an example: let the number of super-classes be $\sqrt{N_c}$ and let each super-class contain $\sqrt{N_c}$ pattern classes. The templet matching may then be performed in two steps. First, the correct super-class is located. On the average, when there is no context information available $\sqrt{N_C}/2$ super-class templets must be checked before the super-class is identified. Next, the templets for the members of the super-class in question are checked. When there is no context information available, $\sqrt{N_C}/2$ templets on the average must be checked before the class-membership is established. In the case of the numerical example mentioned above, the two step procedure would on the average require a total of only $\sqrt{N_C}$ templet matching operations per classification. For N_C large, this is substantially less than the $N_C/2$ operations required with a one step procedure. A two step procedure has for instance been used in a device to recognize 1000 printed Chinese ideographs (Casey and Nagy 1966).

1.5.6 Selection of a Set of p Attributes. In this subsection the general case is considered where the number of attributes to be selected, p, is more than one, and where the attributes are of a more general nature than the measurement of agreement between a pattern and a set of N_C templets. The problem of concern is: how should the designer in practice select an effective subset of p attributes from a large set of N_p attributes? The effectiveness of a set of attributes was defined in Article 1.5.2.1 and it was pointed out that the effectiveness is conditioned on (i) an index of performance, IP, related to the decision procedure used by the designer, and on (ii) "the means for categorization" meaning the device by which the decision space is partitioned. In practice it is usually not too important for the effectiveness which IP is used. The choice of the means for categorization, on the other hand, is crucial for the effectiveness of a set of attributes; e.g., the attribute pair (Ξ_1, Ξ_2) in Figure 1.4 will give perfect separation if and only if the means for categorization can establish a separation surface consisting of two vertical and two

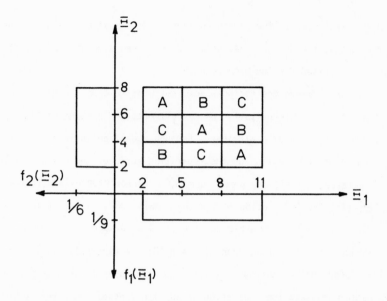

A Bivariate Distribution. The members of Class A are located in the three 3 x 2 rectangles marked A; the tri-modal, bivariate probability density is constant and equal to 1/18. The members of Classes B and C likewise are located in the rectangles marked B and C, their density is also 1/18. The three classes of patterns may be perfectly separated if and only if the separation surface consists (essentially) of four straight lines, $\Xi_1 = 5$, $\Xi_1 = 8$, $\Xi_2 = 4$ and $\Xi_2 = 6$. If the members of all three classes had been distributed each with the density 1/54 over the rectangle with the vertices (2,2), (2,8), (11,8) and (11,2), the classes would have been inseparable with any kind of separation surface. Yet, in both cases the marginal densities $f_1(\Xi_1)$ and $f_2(\Xi_2)$ would be the same for all three classes. This example illustrates the point that even when the marginal distributions for the different classes do overlap much, perfect separation may be possible when the separation surface is compatible with the multivariate distributions.

Fig. 1.4.

horizontal lines. In the remaining part of this subsection it will be assumed that the designer has selected an IP and a means for categorization which are suited for the problem at hand.

In cases where the designer does not want to commit himself to an IP and a means for categorization he may estimate the ranking of the effectiveness of subsets of p attributes through use of an indicator which is independent of the location of the separation surface. The designer could, for instance, use (i) the upper bound of an error probability (Becker 1974), (ii) the information measure G_1 (Lewis 1962; Patrick 1972, Sec. 2-23), or (iii) the symmetric divergence, J_{AB}; G_1 and J_{AB} were mentioned in Subsection 1.5.4, Paragraphs (4) and (5); in particular J_{AB} has been widely used. Notice that when a set of p attributes is used to separate N_C pattern classes the separation of any two classes can never be inferior to the separation which could have been achieved with any subset of the p attributes. Next three different procedures for selecting an effective subset of attributes from a set of N_p attributes will be described; a fourth approach (Akers 1965) will be described in Section 2.5.

Exhaustive Search. If the number of possible subsets, $(N_p!/(p!(N_p -p)!))$, is not too large the value of the IP may be computed in each case. Of all the possible subsets the subset with the largest IP-value is selected and this truly optimum subset is used. For $N_C>2$ and normal distributions with equal covariance matrices a procedure has been used (Chen 1965) where the set of p attributes is so chosen that the minimum symmetric divergence among the $(N_C-1)N_C/2$ pairs of classes is maximized; the purpose of this selection procedure is to obtain a safeguard against the choice of attribute sets that may result in large misrecognition percentages for certain pattern classes. Usually, however, the number of possible subsets is by far too large to permit an exhaustive search.

Sequential Elimination. The IP-value is computed for the (N_p-1) possible subsets of (N_p-1) attributes. The subset with the highest IP-value is retained; let it contain the attributes: $\Xi_1, \ldots, \Xi_{N_p-1}$, the attribute Ξ_{N_p} which had the smallest incremental effectiveness has thus been eliminated. Next the IP is computed for the (N_p-2) subsets obtained by suppressing one of the retained attributes at a time. The attribute with the smallest incremental effectiveness, say Ξ_{N_p-1} is eliminated, etc. The procedure is continued until only p attributes remain; the set of p attributes is then regarded as being if not the optimum at least a near optimum subset of p attributes. A sequential elimination requires fewer computations than an exhaustive search and experimental evidence (Cardillo and Fu 1967, Paragraphs 1 and 2) tends to indicate that approximately the same subset of p attributes will be obtained by either method. The sequential elimination method has been used with the symmetric divergence, J_{AB}, as estimator for effectiveness and under assumption of normal distribution and $N_C=2$ (Marill and Green 1963, Experiment 1).

The Matrix Method. In most practical cases both an exhaustive search and a sequential elimination procedure will require far too much computational effort. Usually the designer has available only a set of N_p density functions (or normalized histograms) for each of the N_C pattern classes. The designer may now proceed as follows:

(i) draw a matrix of size N_C by N_C; the entry at row no. i and column no. j. is called A_{ij}; only the $N_C(N_C-1)/2$ entries in the upper right half will be used;

(ii) list at each entry the names of those (among the N_p) attributes which are effective in separating members of C_i from members of C_j;

(iii) select the p attributes one by one beginning with the attribute mentioned most often in the matrix and continue in a manner which agrees with the index of performance (the designer had only the marginal distributions to start with so a heuristic selection procedure must be excused at this point).

Use of the matrix method has been described in the literature; as an example a model for pattern recognition by Kamentsky and Liu (Kamentsky and Liu 1964) will be briefly reviewed. It is here assumed that all attributes are two-valued functions and $N_C \geq 2$. Two indicators, I and D, are used to quantitatively describe each attribute. I is the average information about class membership given by the attribute just like G_1 (Lewis 1962). When a set of attributes is used there is the possibility that the percentage of misclassifications becomes very large for the members of one of the classes. To overcome this problem the concept of the quantity D is introduced. D_{ij} is defined as the number of attributes that separate members of C_i and C_j "well" in some appropriate sense. With this method the set of p (or fewer) attributes is selected so that the $N_C(N_C-1)/2$ D-values all exceed a certain specified minimum; the designer will try to select the p attributes in a manner so that the smallest D_{ij} becomes as large as possible.

1.6 Decision Procedures and Indices of Performance.

Figure 1.1 illustrates that the receptor maps a pattern into a point in p-dimensional space. Based on the location of the point a decision is made in the categorizer with regard to which of the N_C pattern classes, C_i, i=1, ..., N_C, the pattern presumably belongs to. The designer makes the decision so that a suitable IP is optimized for the design data, the value of the optimized IP indicates the relative performance of the PR.

This subsection describes four methods by which such a decision may
be made. The methods are Bayes' procedure, the minimaxing classification
procedure, the likelihood method and the Neyman-Pearson method. The result
of any of the four decision procedures may be realized through explicit
partitioning of the pattern space. The results of Bayes' procedure and the
likelihood method may also be realized by implicit partitioning. The four
decision procedures mentioned above are well known and widely used. The
designer is of course free to define a new IP say a "mean squared error"-
criterion if that would be more appropriate for the problem at hand
(Watanabe 1972, pp. 575-589; Duda and Hart 1973, Sec. 5.8).

1.6.1 Some Functions Related to the Micro-Regions. The problem of finding
a suitable decision procedure arises in the following manner. In this
section assume that such a large number of representative members of all
N_C pattern classes are available that the N_C multivariate probability
densities can be estimated with great accuracy over the whole p-dimensional
space. This assumption is unrealistic in most cases; e.g., if 8 attributes
each can take 10 discrete values it becomes necessary to estimate N_C probabilities at 10^8 points. In practice the problem may be handled by one of
the methods described in Subsection 1.7.1. Let the space be partitioned
into a very large number, N_M, of very small p-dimensional compartments,
the micro-regions, W_1, W_2, ..., W_k, ..., W_{N_M}. A point that represents a
pattern is assumed to fall in one and only one of the micro-regions; such
a pattern point will be called Ξ. If a point represents a member of C_i, it
is referred to as a C_i-point and it will be called $_i\Xi$. Let the probability
with which a C_i-point falls in micro-region W_k be $P(i)_k$.

$$P(i)_k = P(\Xi \epsilon W_k | \Xi \text{ is a } _i\Xi) \quad\quad ; (1.1)$$

Let $P_{pr}(i)$ be the a priori probability of an unlabeled pattern belonging to pattern class C_i. The probability of an unlabeled pattern being represented by a point that falls in micro-region W_k is then P_k.

$$P_k = \sum_{m=1}^{N_C} P(m)_k \cdot P_{pr}(m) \quad\quad ; (1.2)$$

The sum of the N_M P_k-values, $k = 1, \ldots, N_M$ is unity. Let K_{ij} be the cost of classifying a member of C_i as being a member of C_j. The convention is used that for any given i, K_{ii} is non-positive and the (N_C-1) K_{ij}-values, where $i \neq j$, all are non-negative. To describe the costs of all possible correct and erroneous classifications, a matrix with N_C by N_C entries is needed. When an unlabeled pattern is represented by a point that falls in the micro-region W_k, the pattern will be classified as belonging to one of the N_C classes, say C_i. Sometimes this decision is correct and the cost K_{ii} is incurred. If the pattern belongs to one of the other classes a cost K_{ji} is incurred, $i \neq j$. On the average the cost $(K_i)_k$ is incurred if it is decided that all patterns that are represented by points falling in W_k should be classified as members of C_i.

$$(K_i)_k = \sum_{m=1}^{N_C} P(m)_k \cdot P_{pr}(m) \cdot K_{mi} \quad\quad ; (1.3)$$

$(K_i)_k$ may also be expressed by Equation 1.4.

$$(K_i)_k = E\{\text{classification Cost} | \Xi \epsilon W_k, \text{ all } \Xi \text{ classified as } _i\Xi\} \cdot P_k \quad\quad ; (1.4)$$

1.6.2 Bayes' Procedure. With each class C_i and each micro-region W_k is associated the expected cost of classification $(K_i)_k$. An eminently reasonable rule for classifying an unlabeled pattern that is represented by a point in W_k is to classify it as belonging to the pattern class $i(k)$, for which the average classification cost is as low as possible;

$$(K_{i(k)})_k = \min\{(K_i)_k\}, i \in \{1, ..., N_C\}.$$

This procedure of classifying so as to minimize the expected cost was developed by Thomas Bayes, about two hundred years ago. With this procedure an expected cost R^* is associated with the classification of an unlabeled pattern; R^* can be computed from Equation 1.6, which may be derived in the following manner. Some members of C_j will be classified correctly, namely those for which the corresponding points fall in micro-regions where all points are classified as C_j-points; such micro-regions have $i(k) = j$. The remaining members of C_j will be misclassified in one or more of the (N_C-1) possible ways. Equation 1.5 determines the expected cost, $R(j)$, of classifying a pattern, given that the pattern belongs to C_j. $R(j)$ should not be confused with $(K_j)_k$ which was defined by Equation 1.3. N_M is the number of micro-regions.

$$R(j) = \sum_{k=1}^{N_M} P(j)_k \cdot K_{ji(k)} \qquad ; (1.5)$$

It is now clear that "Bayes' risk", R^*, the minimized, expected cost of classifying an unlabeled pattern, must be the weighted average of $R(j)$ as indicated by Equation 1.6.

$$R^* = \sum_{j=1}^{N_C} R(j) \cdot P_{pr}(j) \qquad\qquad ; (1.6)$$

When Bayes' procedure is used "minus one times the average cost of classifying a pattern" would constitute a reasonable index of performance.

Usually not all $R(i)$, $i \in \{1, \ldots, N_C\}$, have the same value. Let it be assumed that the following relationship exists:

$$R(1) \geq R(2) \geq \ldots \geq R(N_C).$$

Recalling Equation 1.6 the following relationship is seen to be valid.

$$R(1) \geq R^* \geq R(N_C).$$

1.6.3 The Minimaxing Classification Procedure. If the a priori probabilities for some reason change from the given values, $P_{pr}(i)$, the designer must redesign the categorizer, meaning that he must find new values for $i(k)$, $k=1, \ldots, N_M$. In case the classification of points in each micro-region has to be maintained by the designer after the change of a priori probabilities, the average classification cost presumably will change. Assuming that $R(1) \geq R^* \geq R(N_C)$ the cost could increase to $R(1)$ if all unlabeled patterns now belong to C_1, and it could decrease to $R(N_C)$ if all unlabeled patterns belong to C_{N_C}. If the designer has no information about the values of $P_{pr}(1), \ldots, P_{pr}(N_C)$ he cannot afford to guess; he will want to classify in such a manner that the largest possible average classification cost has been minimized. To do this the designer will make

use of the minimaxing classification procedure, a procedure that will now
be described in principle. All patterns that are represented by points
falling in W_k will be classified as belonging to C_{i_k}, $i_k \epsilon \{1, 2, \ldots, N_C\}$.
i_k will be defined shortly; i_k should not be confused with the minimizing
quantity $i(k)$ from Bayes' procedure. Any classification rule may be described by an array of N_M i_k-values; let $(i_1, \ldots, i_{N_M})$ illustrate the
array. The average cost of classifying members of C_j is $B(j)$, $j=1, \ldots, N_C$;
$B(j)$ is defined by Equation 1.7 for the minimaxing classification procedure. $B(j)$ may be considered a counterpart to $R(j)$, Equation 1.5.

$$B(j) \quad = \quad \sum_{k=1}^{N_M} P(j)_k \cdot K_{ji_k} \qquad\qquad ; \ (1.7)$$

The minimzxing procedure consists of finding the array $(i_1, \ldots, i_{N_M})$
for which the maximum $\{B(j)\}$ is minimized, $j \epsilon \{1, \ldots, N_C\}$.

$$\underset{j}{\text{minimax}}\{B(j)\} = \underset{(i_1, \ldots, i_{N_M})}{\text{minimum}} \quad \{\underset{j}{\text{maximum}} \ \{\sum_{k=1}^{N_M} P(j)_k \cdot K_{ji_k}\}\} \qquad ; \ (1.8)$$

Equation 1.8 shows how $\underset{j}{\text{minimax}}\{B(j)\}$ in principle may be found by (i)
changing one of the N_M i_k-values at a time and by (ii) always making the
change in such a manner that the largest of the N_C average classification
costs is reduced. In the general case there may be several, local minimax
values of different magnitude. When $N_C = 2$, the result of the minimaxing
procedure may be expressed in closed form (Selin 1965, Chapter 2). It is
possible to mix the Bayes' and the minimaxing decision procedures so that
one minimaxes to avoid catastrophically high risks and minimizes the remaining average risk (Lehmann 1959, Section 1.6).

38

When the minimaxing procedure is used $(-\text{maximum}\{B(j)\})$ would con-
$\qquad\qquad\qquad\qquad j$
stitute a reasonable index of performance.

1.6.4 The Likelihood Method.

In many cases the values of the N_C^2 possible classification costs, and the N_C a priori probabilities are unknown to the designer. In such situations only the N_C values of $P(m)_k$ are available; $P(m)_k$ is the probability of a C_m-point falling in the micro-region W_k rather than in one of the (N_M-1) other micro-regions, $P(m)_k$ was defined by Equation 1.1. A more or less obvious basis for a decision rule is given by what is called the likelihood principle. The principle states that an unlabeled pattern that is represented by a point located in W_k should be classified as being a member of the class C_{ℓ_k} for which classmembership has the greatest likelihood; ℓ_k is defined by Equation 1.9.

$$P(\ell_k)_k = \underset{m}{\text{maximum}}\{P(m)_k\}, \ m\epsilon\{1, \ldots, N_C\} \qquad\qquad ; (1.9)$$

If Class no. s happens to be C_{ℓ_k}, the (N_C-1) likelihood ratios $P(s)_k/P(t)_k$, $t=1, \ldots, N_C$, $t \neq s$, will all be somewhat larger than unity. If the (N_C-1) likelihood ratios are computed for any of the other (N_C-1) classes at least one of the likelihood ratios will be less than unity. It may consequently be determined from the likelihood ratios which class has the highest likelihood of classmembership. Algorithms for approximating likelihood ratio computations have been described in the literature (Sebestyen 1962, Section 4.3). The likelihood method and Bayes' procedure become identical in the often encountered case where (i) all N_C a priori probabilities are equal, $P_{pr}(j) = 1/N_C$, (ii) all N_C correct classification costs K_{ii} are equal, and (iii) all $N_C (N_C-1)/2$ misclassification costs K_{ij}, $i \neq j$, are equal.

When the likelihood method is used the percentage of correctly classified patterns would be a reasonable index of performance.

1.6.5 The Neyman-Pearson Method. When as before the a priori probabilities and the classification costs are not known to the designer and
furthermore $N_C = 2$, a special procedure becomes possible. Classification
of points in the N_M micro-regions may then be made according to the
Neyman-Pearson criterion where the idea is to keep the percentage of misclassified C_1-patterns at some prescribed level, $100 \cdot R_{N-P}\%$, $0 \leq R_{N-P} \leq 1$,
while the percentage of misclassified C_2-patterns is minimized (Davenport
and Root 1958, Section 14-3). The procedure is used when misclassification
of C_1-patterns is particularly undesirable. The decision procedure will
in practice consist of the following steps. (The procedure is not restricted to the familiar case, p=1).

(i) First the likelihood ratio $L_k = P(2)_k/P(1)_k$, k=1, ..., N_M, is computed for each of the N_M micro-regions.

(ii) The micro-region for which L_k is smallest, let it be W_1, is classified as a C_1 region and it is checked that the following inequality holds:
$1-P(1)_1 \geq R_{N-P}$.

(iii) Of the remaining micro-regions, the one with the by now lowest
value of L_k, is classified as a C_1 region, let it be W_2. It is checked
that $1-P(1)_1 - P(1)_2 \geq R_{N-P}$.

(iv) In this manner repeatedly the micro-region with the lowest L_k-value
is classified as a C_1 region. At each step it is checked that the percentage of C_1-patterns that thus far has not been classified does exceed
$100 \cdot R_{N-P}\%$.

(v) Sooner or later micro-regions containing $100 \cdot (1-R_{N-P})\%$ of the C_1-patterns have been classified as C_1-regions. The remaining micro-regions are then all classified as C_2-regions.

By this procedure the N_M micro-regions have been divided so that while $100 \cdot R_{N-P}\%$ of the C_1-patterns are misclassified the least number of C_2-patterns are misclassified.

When the Neyman-Pearson method is used and R_{N-P} is specified, <u>the percentage of correctly classified C_2-patterns would constitute a reasonable index of performance.</u>

1.6.6 Three Practical Difficulties. What has been obtained this far in this section is development of some techniques by which all unlabeled patterns, which are represented by points in the micro-region W_k, may be classified as being members of one and only one of the N_C possible pattern classes. With these techniques so to say a class membership has been assigned to each micro-region. The next step in the development of a realistic decision procedure is the fusion of all adjacent micro-regions to which the same class, C_i has been assigned. By repeated fusing of the micro-regions a few large regions, macro-regions, will be obtained; with each macro-region is associated a class membership. In case (i) a description of the p-dimensional surface that separate the macro-regions and (ii) the class number, i, assigned to each macro-region could be stored in the categorizer, a categorizer would have been obtained that was optimum in the sense chosen by the designer. In practice the approach described above - the construction of an "optimal recognition function" (Marill and Green 1960) - seldomly works out for three reasons.

(1) There are usually too few representative patterns available to deter-

mine the N_C multivariate distributions (without making assumptions about the distributions, a possibility which has not been considered in this section but will be discussed in Subsection 1.7.1).

(2) There is usually not enough time and funding to process the many patterns even if they were available.

(3) Unless the separation surfaces are of fairly simple shape or the dimensionality, p, of the space is very low, the number of constants needed to describe the surfaces easily becomes so large that the information storage in the categorizer presents problems; in the extreme case where the micro-regions do not fuse at all it becomes necessary to store the class membership for each of the N_M micro-regions.

In Section 1.7 it will be described how categorizers are designed in practice or in other words, how the p-dimensional separation surface, or an approximation hereof, may be determined in spite of the three obstacles listed above.

1.7 Categorizer Design.

The answer to the three problems described in Subsection 1.6.6 clearly is, to partition the pattern space in a manner which requires the determination of fairly few constants. The few constants usually can be evaluated from the available representative patterns (which in most cases are limited in number) with a reasonable effort in time and funding, and the values of the few constants can be stored in memories of realistic size. This section about categorizer design is divided into four parts, one about methods for explicit partitioning of the pattern space, Subsection 1.7.2, and one about methods for implicit partitioning of the pattern space, Subsection 1.7.3. In both parts some methods the so called non-parametric methods, will be mentioned where the designer makes no assumption about the distributions in pattern space of the members of the N_C classes. With the remaining methods, the parametric methods, the designer in some manner makes use of known or assumed distributions. In Subsection 1.7.4 several methods are described for categorization of members from more than two classes, $N_C > 2$. As a preliminary it is in Subsection 1.7.1 considered how the N_C multivariate density functions may be estimated.

1.7.1 Estimation of a Multivariate Density Function. By using p attributes rather than one in the receptor, the descriptive power of the receptor is enhanced substantially. However, at the same time a new problem has been created in the following manner. Whereas one-dimensional histograms usually can be obtained in practice, p-dimensional histograms are not available in most realistic situations because their computation and subsequent storage become impractical. If p, for instance, equals 10 and each attribute can take 8 values, there are 8^{10}, or more than one billion, possible combinations of attribute values. It is usually not possible in practice to estimate the multivariate density functions for each of the N_C classes with any precision over such a space; (for moderate values of p it may still be possible to obtain reasonable p-dimensional histograms (Patrick 1972, page 34). It consequently becomes necessary to make assumptions about the form of the density functions in some manner. When a suitable assumption can be introduced only relatively few constants have to be estimated before the density function can be estimated. Some examples will now be presented of the kinds of assumptions which are used by designers. The multivariate density function for members of C_j is called $P_j(\Xi)$ =

$P_j(\Xi_1, \Xi_2, \ldots, \Xi_p)$. The univariate density function for values of attribute Ξ_i is called ${}^iP_j(\Xi_i)$, $i = 1, \ldots, p$; the designer usually has enough patterns to estimate these p marginal densities with sufficient accuracy for each of the N_C classes.

Certain Higher Order Statistical Dependencies are Disregarded. An often used (and strong) assumption is that of statistical independence for all p attributes; in this very simple case $P_j(\Xi)$ becomes the product of the p (reasonably well defined), marginal densities.

$$P_j(\Xi) = {}^1P_j(\Xi_1) \cdot {}^2P_j(\Xi_2) \cdot \ldots \cdot {}^pP_j(\Xi_p) \qquad\qquad ; (1.10)$$

Sometimes the designer for physical reasons can assume that certain groups of attributes are statistically independent (this is a weaker assumption than the one above); e.g., a first group could be the first 3 attributes and a second group the remaining (p-3) attributes. In such a case $P_j(\Xi)$ can be written in the following simpler form.

$$P_j(\Xi) = {}^\alpha P_j(\Xi_1, \Xi_2, \Xi_3) \cdot {}^\beta P_j(\Xi_4, \ldots, \Xi_p) \qquad\qquad ; (1.11)$$

A numerical example will illustrate the advantage of the decomposition. Assume that (i) all attributes are three valued, (ii) p = 6, (iii) N_C = 2, and (iv) the number of design data patterns from Classes 1 and 2 is $M_{1D} = M_{2D} = 3^6 = 729$. If so, the designer can estimate ${}^\alpha P_1$, ${}^\beta P_1$, ${}^\alpha P_2$ and ${}^\beta P_2$; each of the four densities will consist of $3^3 = 27$ discrete probabilities which may be estimated reasonably well given 729 pattern points. If the designer does not make use of the decomposition he will have to estimate P_1 and P_2 directly, P_1 and P_2 do both consist of $3^6 =$ 729 discrete probabilities; the 729 (rather than 27) estimates are still based on only 729 pattern points. It should now be clear that the product of the $^\alpha P_1$- and $^\beta P_2$- estimates will be at least as accurate and probably much more accurate than a direct P_1-estimate; also the product of the $^\alpha P_2$- and $^\beta P_2$-estimates can be expected to be substantially more accurate than a direct P_2-estimate. The more the designer can decompose P_j, the easier and more accurate the estimation of P_j becomes.

The case where all p attributes are two-valued functions has received particular attention; techniques are available for the approximation of $P_j(\Xi)$ to reduce storage requirements (Duda and Hart 1973, Sec. 4.9), $P_j(\Xi)$ may for instance be approximated with dependence trees (Bell 1974) or Markow chains (Chow 1966; Ma 1974).

A Specific Functional Form is Assumed. Sometimes the designer knows (or guesses) what the functional form of $P_j(\Xi)$ is. The functional form could be Gaussian, Pearson Type II or Type VII (Cooper 1964), uniform density inside a hypersphere, etc. In such cases the designer usually pools the design data for each class and estimates the values of the parameters of interest, e.g., for a Gaussian distribution the important parameters are the mean vector and the covariance matrix for each class. In rare cases the designer in addition has statistical information about the parameter values he is about to estimate and becomes able to estimate the values in a sequential fashion. E.g., the designer may know a priori that the density is Gaussian with zero mean and that the inverse of the (unknown) covariance matrix has a Wishart density (Patrick 1972, Sec. 2-10). Having measured the attribute values for the first representative pattern he is able to compute the a posteriori probability density for the inverse covariance matrix, the density turns out also to have the form of a Wishart density (but it is more concentrated than the previous one). In such special cases where

the a priori and a posteriori densities for the unknown parameters have
the same functional form (which is the exception, see Patrick 1972, Sec.
2-11), it becomes possible to estimate the parameter values by repeating the procedure; each member of C_j in the design data group is used to
obtain a new and more concentrated density for the unknown parameter
values. When all the representative C_j members have been used, the expected values of the parameters are used as true values in the $P_j(\Xi)$-density
function.

Truncated Orthonormal Expansion. Based on his knowledge (or expectations) about $P_j(\Xi)$, the designer selects a suitable orthonormal system,
$\Phi_1(\Xi)$, $\Phi_2(\Xi)$, etc., and decides on how many terms, say n, he will use for
his approximation of $P_j(\Xi)$ (Patrick 1972, Sec. 2-22). The remaining questions are: what weights w_1, w_2, ..., w_n should the designer use to make
$\sum_{i=1}^{n} w_i \Phi_i(\Xi)$ a best approximation of $P_j(\Xi)$, say, in the mean square error
sense, and what is the rate of convergence (Wagner 1968)? The answers
may be obtained by stochastic approximation (Robbins and Monro 1951; Mendel and Fu 1970, Chapters 9 and 10; Patrick 1972, Sec. 2-19 or related
techniques, where the weight vector $w = (w_1, ..., w_n)$ is determined by an
iterative procedure. Also in the case of a nonlinearly evolving nonstation-
ary environment such techniques have been useful (Yau and Schumpert 1968).

1.7.2 Explicit Partitioning of the Pattern Space. This subsection is
divided as follows. First some widely used separation surfaces of simple
shape are mentioned, after which the need for such simple surfaces is
established. Finally in Articles 1.7.2.3 and 1.7.2.4 parametric and non-
parametric methods are described for locating such simple surfaces in an
optimum manner.

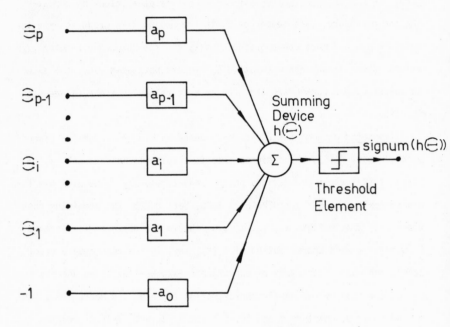

The threshold logic unit, TLU. The summer generates the function

$$h(\Xi) = a_0 + \sum_{i=1}^{p} a_i \Xi_i.$$

The threshold element generates a +1 signal for $h(\Xi)>0$ and a -1 signal for $h(\Xi)<0$; the signal is signum$\{h(\Xi)\}$. signum$\{0\}$ may be arbitrarily defined as being +1 rather than -1.

Figure 1.5

1.7.2.1 Separation Surfaces of Simple Shape. When the partitioning is
explicit, use is made of separation surfaces of simple shape, e.g., qua-
drics (which illustrate second order equations), orthotopes (which are
hyperspace-analogs of three dimensional boxes), and above all hyperplanes
(which are planes in hyperspace); the location of such surfaces is determined by the values of fairly few constants. The equation for a hyperplane is $h(\Xi) = 0$ where

$$h(\Xi) = a_0 + \sum_{i=1}^{p} a_i \, \Xi_i \qquad\qquad ; (1.12)$$

The (p+1) constants a_0, a_1, ..., a_p represent p pieces of information.
Any point on the positive side of the hyperplane has a positive value of
$h(\Xi)$; any point on the negative side has a negative value of $h(\Xi)$. The
location of a point with respect to a hyperplane may therefore be determined from the sign of $h(\Xi)$; e.g., the sign of a_0 indicates on which side
of the plane the origin is. The function signum $\{h(\Xi)\}$, or sgn$\{h(\Xi)\}$, may
be generated by a threshold logic unit, TLU, as shown in Figure 1.5. The
TLU has been used alone as categorizer, it has also been used as the ele-
mental building block of more elaborate categorizers, e.g., layered
machines (Nilsson 1965, Chapter 6) which are networks of interconnected
TLUs and which include committee mchines. A committee machine is a PR
consisting of an odd number of TLUs, each of which has one "vote", the
PR makes decisions according to the majority of the TLU votes. Simple
separation surfaces may be obtained by cascading TLU units as indicated
by an example in Figure 1.6.

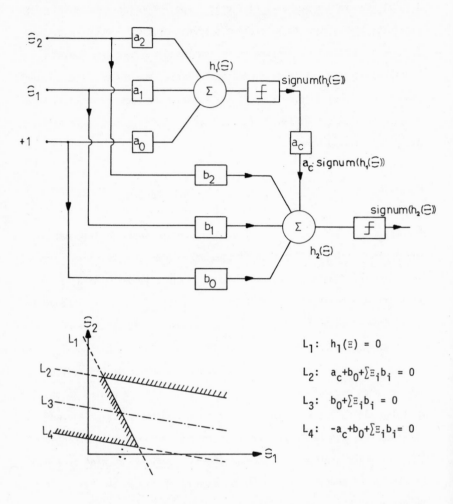

L_1: $h_1(\Xi) = 0$

L_2: $a_c + b_0 + \sum \Xi_i b_i = 0$

L_3: $b_0 + \sum \Xi_i b_i = 0$

L_4: $-a_c + b_0 + \sum \Xi_i b_i = 0$

The figure presents an example of how a nonlinear separation surface may be generated by cascading threshold logic units. Two TLUs and two attributes Ξ_1 and Ξ_2 are used. The heavy zig-zag line indicates the nonlinear separation surface in the (Ξ_1, Ξ_2)-plane. Above the zig-zag line $h_2(\Xi)$ is positive, below the line $h_2(\Xi)$ is negative. The equations for the four lines, L_1, L_2, L_3, and L_4, are listed above.

Figure 1.6

1.7.2.2 The Need for Surfaces of Simple Shape. The easiest way to illustrate the need is by way of a numerical example. Consider a problem with 2 classes, Class A and Class B, where the designer uses 50 attributes and where all 50 density functions look like Figure 1.3. Clearly the 50-variate density function for Class A members may be anywhere from trimodal to 3^{50}-modal and the density function for Class B members may be anywhere from bi-modal to 2^{50}-modal. The separation surface obtained by 50 sets of 4 thresholds like those in Figure 1.3 will probably be suboptimal. The optimum separation surface will in all likelihood be highly convoluted so the surface will be difficult to locate and to store. In contra distinction to this situation the designer should have little trouble finding an optimum (or near-optimum) separation surface of simple shape if he has 50 attributes like the one illustrated in Figure 1.2.

The need for separation surfaces of simple shape give rise to the question: what can the designer do to make such surfaces optimum (or near optimum) and in particular what can he do to avoid that highly convoluted surfaces become optimum? It is in general so that the surface which is needed to separate disjointed classes (and to a lesser degree classes with multimodal distributions) from each other is of a more complicated shape than the surface needed to separate classes with unimodal distributions. Therefore, the designer should consider dividing any class with a multimodal distribution into subclasses with unimodal distributions. There are two steps which the designer can take to achieve such a decomposition. (i) The designer should see if the members of the class in question, C_i, do actually come from distinct subclasses, $C_{i,1}$, $C_{i,2}$, etc., which are generically different. If so, the designer should consider working with the subclasses rather than with C_i. E.g., C_i could be the class of typewritten capital A letters, $C_{i,1}$ could be Pica capital A letters, $C_{i,2}$ could be Elite capital A letters, etc. Membership in C_i will after the division of the class be decided in the last stage of the categorizer in the following manner. If the unlabeled pattern is identified as being a member of one (or more) of the C_i-subclasses and of none of the other (N_C-1) classes, the pattern is classified as being a member of C_i.

(ii) A second step the designer can take is to find the "Clusters", meaning locations in p-dimensional space with high densities of C_i-patterns. This can be achieved with suitable cluster seeking procedures (Watanabe 1972, pp. 291-311; Patrick 1972, Sections 5-4 and 5-5; Duda and Hart 1973, Chap. 6; Nagy 1968, Part IV). Patterns that belong to cluster no. 1, 2, etc., are considered to belong to the subclasses $C_{i,1}$ $C_{i,2}$, etc.. The designer can also determine the clusters by one of the methods for non-supervised classification of patterns (Fralick 1967; Meisel 1972, Chap. VIII; Patrick 1972, Chap. 5). If the unlabeled pattern is identified as being a member of one (or more) of the C_i-subclasses and of none of the other (N_C-1) classes the pattern is classified as being a member of C_i.

It is necessary in practice to use separation surfaces of simple shape. Fortunately, there are a number of important cases where the optimum form of the separation surface actually is simple; examples of such cases will be presented in Article 1.7.2.3. Sometimes the designer wants to separate two classes of pattern points having distributions of unknown forms. In such cases the designer may select a separation surface of suitable but simple shape and locate it in an optimum fashion in pattern space; this procedure will be discussed in Article 1.7.2.4.

1.7.2.3 Parametric Training Methods. Consider the case where the functional forms of the N_C multivariate densities are known. E.g., the members of C_i could have a multivariate Gaussian density. When the functional forms of the N_C densities are known, the functional form of the optimum separation surface can be computed so as to optimize a specified IP. By parametric training methods are understood methods that use the design data to estimate the values of the parameters for the computed optimum separation surface. The estimates are often said to be obtained from the design data by a "training procedure". These estimates are then later used as optimum values when the categorizer is realized in hardware or software. Two important cases will now be presented.

Separation Surfaces of Optimum Form. Let the p attributes have a multivariate, Gaussian or Pearson Type II, or Pearson Type VII, density for both members of C_1 and members of C_2; in this case the optimum separation surface is a quadric (Cooper 1964). The location of the quadric may be determined by the two mean vectors and the two covariance or scaling matrices, all of which can be estimated from the design data. Under special conditions the quadric reduces to two hyperplanes or only one hyperplane. E.g., if two multivariate, Gaussian distributions have the same covariance matrix the optimum separation surface is a single hyperplane (Cooper 1964).

Separation Surfaces of Suboptimal Form. In case the optimum separation surface is too convoluted the designer may compute the optimum location of a separation surface of given (and simpler) functional form. By using a suboptimal form of separation surface the designer accepts a loss in maximized IP-value to gain a simpler categorizer implementation and a simpler (and maybe faster) categorization procedure. An example of a suboptimal separation surface is a hyperplane used (instead of a quadric) to separate two Gaussian, multivariate distributions with unequal covariance matrices (Anderson and Bahadur 1962).

1.7.2.4 Non-Parametric Training Methods. Non-parametric training methods are applied when no assumptions can be made about the N_C multivariate distributions. In this situation some functional form is assumed for the separation surface such as the linear, quadric, or piecewise linear form (Patrick 1972, pp. 268-277); the designer's choice of form will depend on his expectations with regard to the modalities of the N_C densities. The functions have unspecified coefficients (often called weights), the values of which are adjusted by the designer in such a manner that the separation surface performs as well as possible on the design data. The coefficient adjustment is commonly referred to as training. If the members of two classes can be separated by a hyperplane they are said to be linearly separable. Non-parametric training procedures for the "linearly separable" and "not linearly separable" case will be discussed followed by two notes on linear separation.

Linearly Separable Patterns. It is desired to find a hyperplane that separates M_{AD} representative pattern points belonging to Class A from M_{BD} pattern points belonging to Class B. It is known a priori that the patterns are linearly separable. Besides the linear programming approach several training procedures are available by which a suitable hyperplane always can be located after a finite number of iterations. The methods have been carefully described in Chapter 5 of Duda and Hart 1973 and compared in Table 5-1. Numerical examples of such procedures are available in the literature (Nilsson 1965, Table 4.1; Nagy 1968, Table II). The procedures are called error-correcting because the location of the hyperplane is continually being adjusted so as to correct the erroneous classifications of the representative patterns. It gives a substantial saving in computer time if the starting position of the hyperplane is selected with care; if the members of both classes are unimodally distributed with centroids M_A and M_B, a reasonable starting position would be one where the hyperplane bisects the line connecting M_A with M_B.

The ease with which M_{AD} points are separated from M_{BD} points by a hyperplane obviously depends on the dimensionality p; this matter will now be discussed. The M_{AD} plus M_{BD} pattern points in p-dimensional space are usually in "general position". A set of points is said to be in general position when no subset of (p+1) points lies on a (p-1) dimensional hyperplane. Let it be <u>assumed</u> that all the points are in general position and arbitrarily located in the p-dimensional space. Then the points can be separated correctly (i) with 100% probability when $M_{AD} + M_{BD} \leq p+1$, (ii) with more than 50% probability when $M_{AD} + M_{BD} < 2p$, (iii) with 50% probability when $M_{AD} + M_{BD} = 2p$, and (iv) with less than 50% probability when $M_{AD} + M_{BD} > 2p$. The change in probability as a function of $(M_{AD}+M_{BD})/p$ is very pronounced at the 50% level in particular for larger values of p (Duda and Hart 1973, Figure 3.4). It consequently becomes natural to define the capacity of a hyperplane as 2p or twice the number of degrees of freedom, (Duda and Hart 1973, Art. 3.8.3). If the hyperplane can separate more than 2p patterns correctly, and p is moderately large (say more than seven), it indicates that the members of both classes "cluster" well. The existence of clusters again indicates that the p attributes have been well chosen.

<u>Patterns Which are Not Linearly Separable</u>. It is desired to find a hyperplane that separates representative pattern points from two classes,

Classes A and B, while optimizing a specified IP. No assumptions are made about the representative pattern points being linearly separable. This problem has been studied and answers have been obtained which are applicable when the number of misclassified samples are used to measure the performance of the hyperplane or other IPs are used such as the "Perception Criterion Function",(Duda and Hart 1973, Sec. 5.5). The answers take the form of computer programs, as an example the Akers program will be described in Section 2.5. Committee machines have also been used successfully to solve problems of this kind (Nilsson 1965, Sections 6.2, 6.3 and 6.4). The special case where the p attributes all are two-valued functions has received considerable interest and has been surveyed (Winder 1963).

First Note. Consider a problem where the weight and the height of the patterns have been found to be two effective attributes, Ξ_1 and Ξ_2. Clearly the effectiveness of the attributes is independent on whether the height is measured in inches or miles and whether the weight is measured in pounds or stones. In either case the optimally located hyperplanes will give preceisely the same performance although the attributes have been weighted differently; a_1 and a_2 in Equation 1.12 will be different. There is consequently in general no reason to believe that the attributes which are weighted heavily (those with high a-values) are more effective than the attributes with low weight values.

Second Note. Assume that the designer has found the optimum location for a hyperplane which separates Class A points from Class B points. The designer may now want to perform a linear transformation of pattern space to improve the clustering of Class A points and the clustering of Class B points. During the transformation the hyperplane is changed into a surface of the same functional form namely a new hyperplane. The points which were

on opposite sides of the plane before the transformation remain on opposite sides after the transformation. The performance of the (optimum) plane
is precisely the same before and after the transformation; the transformation may result in better clustering but it does not result in fewer
misclassified pattern points. A transformation may improve the PR performance in situations where the "post-transformation optimum separation surface of realizable form" corresponds to a "pre-transformation separation
surface" of a convoluted form which the designer cannot (or does not want
to) realize; transformations which lead to better PR performance will
often include folding in some form.

Some Other Methods. For the sake of completeness it should be mentioned that some simpler classification schemes (Sebestyen 1962, Section
5.1) such as "Correlation with Stored References" and "Proximity to
Nearest Regression Plane" or "Nearest-Class-Mean Classification" also
lead to separation surfaces consisting of hyperplanes. The different
methods have been illustrated by numerical examples in Nagy 1968, Table
1 and Figure 2.

If each attribute can take only a few distinct values, it is possible
to use a decision tree evaluating the attributes sequentially until a
decision can be made, or to use Boolean functions (Becker and Nielsen
1972) in the categorizer but such methods have been reported only rarely
in the literature. The reason is probably that the two methods are not
well suited for separation of populations with overlapping distributions
and populations that are described by representative members only.

Hardware Implementation. Several machines, special purpose computers,
have been built, by which the adjusting of the separation surface coefficients may take place in hardware; e.g., the Perceptron (Rosenblatt 1962;

Minsky and Papert 1969), Adaline (Widrow et al. 1963), the Learning Matrix, (Steinbuch and Widrow 1966), Demo-1 (Patrick 1972, Art. 5-5.4), and AQVAL/1 (Michalski 1973).

1.7.3 Implicit Partitioning of the Pattern Space. This subsection is divided into two parts. In the first part, Article 1.7.3.1, nearest-neighbor-pattern classification is discussed. In the rest of the subsection different forms of discriminant functions are described. In Article 1.7.3.2 the equivalence of discriminant functions and separation surfaces is explained. Next two methods for non-parametric design of discriminant functions are presented. Finally, in Article 1.7.3.6, parametric training of discriminant functions is discussed.

1.7.3.1 Nearest-Neighbor-Pattern Classification. The nearest neighbor decision rule (Patrick 1972, Sec. 4-3; Duda and Hart 1973, Sec. 4.6) assigns to an unlabeled pattern point the classmembership of the nearest of a set of previously classified pattern points. The rule is independent of the N_C underlying multivariate distributions, it is a non-parametric categorization rule. Let the probability of misclassifying a pattern with this rule be called R_{NN} and with Bayes' procedure be called R^* (Bayes' procedure requires complete knowledge of the underlying statistics). In the case where a large number of design data is available it may be shown (Duda and Hart 1973, Eq. 28) that:

$$R^* \leq R_{NN} \leq R^* (2-N_C R^*/(N_C-1)) \qquad\qquad ; (1.13)$$

In other words: when a large number of representative pattern points

from the N_C classes can be stored and the one closest to the unlabeled
point can be identified, then the probability of error with this procedure
is less than $2R^*$. The method is intuitively appealing but it suffers from
the shortcoming that it is difficult both (i) to store a large number of
points and to compute the many distances among which the smallest is desired or (ii) to find the "minimal consistent subset" of correctly classified pattern points (Hart 1968) which will perform as well as the original
large set of points.

1.7.3.2 Discriminant Functions and Separation Surfaces. Any separation
surface can be defined implicitly by a set of N_C functions, $g_i(\Xi) =$
$g_i(\Xi_1, \ldots, \Xi_p)$, i=1, ..., N_C. These functions, which are scalar and
single-valued, are called discriminant functions. They have the property
that $g_m(\Xi) > g_n(\Xi)$ for m,n = 1, ..., N_C, m ≠ n, whenever a pattern point Ξ
is located in a C_m-region; a C_m-region is a region in the p-dimensional
decision space where it is decided to classify all points as being representative of members of Class C_m. The N_C discriminant functions may be
generated in many ways; when Bayes' procedure is used one possible approach
is for each micro-region to use minus one times the N_C $(K_i)_k$-values from
Equation 1.3, Subsection 1.6.1 as function values. Each discriminant may
be illustrated by a surface in a (p+1)-dimensional space obtained by adding
a g-axis to the p-dimensional decision space. The implicitly defined separation surface coincides with the projection on the p-dimensional decision
space of the loci of points in (p+1)-dimensional space where the two
highest valued of the N_C discriminant functions have the same value
(Nilsson 1965, Figure 1.3). When a set of N_C discriminant functions is
known, it is consequently possible to locate the separation surface. If

the separation surface is known, it is possible to determine infinitely many sets of N_C discriminant functions by following the two guidelines. (1) For any pattern point Ξ inside a C_m-region the N_C discriminant functions can take any desired values as long as $g_m(\Xi) > g_n(\Xi)$ for $m,n = 1, \ldots, N_C$, $m \neq n$. (2) For any point Ξ on the separation surface in an area where the surface separates a C_m-region from a C_n-region the N_C discriminant functions can take any desired values as long as $g_m(\Xi) = g_n(\Xi) > g_k(\Xi)$, k, m, $n = 1, \ldots, N_C$, $n \neq m \neq k \neq n$. Consequently, it is seen that <u>just as a set of</u> <u>N_C discriminant functions determines the separation surface, the separation</u> <u>surface determines an infinite number of possible sets of N_C discriminant</u> <u>functions.</u>

1.7.3.3 Categorization Using N_C Discriminants.

The categorizer may be designed so that it uses N_C discriminant functions rather than the expression for the separation surface. If so, the categorizer consists of (1) N_C blocks where the values of the N_C discriminant functions, $g_i(\Xi)$, are computed for the unlabeled pattern Ξ (the N_C computations are often performed in parallel) followed by (2) a block, the maximum selector, where it is decided which discriminant function has the highest value. The index number of that function is then presented as the result of the categorization. When each of the $g_i(\Xi)$-functions is a linear function of Ξ_1, $\Xi_2, \ldots, \Xi_p$, the machine is said to be a linear machine (Nilsson 1965, Section 2.3).

The form of one of the N_C functions may be chosen arbitrarily. E.g., if $(g_i(\Xi) - g_1(\Xi))$ is used instead of $g_i(\Xi)$, $i = 1, \ldots, N_C$, it is seen that $g_1(\Xi) = 0$ for all Ξ-values. A pattern, Ξ, is then classified as being a member of Class 1 if $(g_i(\Xi) - g_1(\Xi)) < 0$, $i = 2, 3, \ldots, N_C$. With this procedure one of the N_C discriminant function generators can be saved; for $N_C = 2$ one discriminant function will suffice, this situation is encountered quite frequently in the literature.

A number of possible discriminant functions have been discussed in the literature (Duda and Hart 1973, Sec. 2.5; Patrick 1972, Sec. 4-14). The most popular function is the linear discriminant function g_{i_L}.

$$g_{i_L}(\Xi) = c_{i0} + c_{i1} \cdot \Xi_1 + \ldots + c_{ip} \cdot \Xi_p \qquad ; (1.14)$$

This function is simple to implement in hardware with a summing circuit. Two logical extensions "the piecewise linear discriminant function" and the "Polynomial discriminant function" (Patrick 1972, Sec. 4-14) have also received attention. The ϕ-machine is a powerful method for generating linear discriminants, it will be described next (Meisel 1972, Sections 4.9 and 5.5).

1.7.3.4 The ϕ-Machine. Let $\phi_j = \phi_j(\Xi_1, \ldots, \Xi_p)$, $j=1, \ldots, d$, be a real-valued measurement function. Consider a machine that first computes the values of the d ϕ-functions for a specified pattern point, secondly selects the largest of the N_C discriminants ϕ_i, $i=1, \ldots, N_C$, defined by Equation 1.15, and finally announces the index number of the discriminant as the classification of the pattern. The $(d+1) \cdot N_C$ quantities in Equation 1.15, $b_{i,j}$, $j=0, 1, \ldots, d$, are coefficients which can be adjusted during training.

$$\phi_i = b_{i,0} + \sum_{j=1}^{d} b_{i,j} \cdot \phi_j, \; i=1, \ldots, N_C \qquad ; (1.15)$$

Such a machine which uses Φ_i functions as discriminants is called a Φ-machine (Nilsson 1965, Section 2.11). Notice the similarity in the form of the expressions for a linear discriminant, $g_{i_L}(\Xi)$, Equation 1.14, and Φ_i, Equation 1.15; $g_{i_L}(\Xi)$ and Φ_i are both linear functions of a set of adjustable coefficients. The Φ-machine has consequently the advantages of a linear machine meaning that it is simple to train non-parametrically; this property was mentioned in Article 1.7.2.4. But thanks to the computation of the ϕ-functions, the Φ-machine is more powerful than a linear machine, which just selects the maximum of $g_{i_L}(\Xi)$, $i=1, \ldots, N_C$. E.g., if $\phi_j = (\Xi_j - c_j)^2$ where c_j is a non-adjustable constant, $j=1, \ldots, p$, E-quation 1.15 describes a quadric surface; a quadric surface clearly is a more powerful discriminant than a hyperplane illustrating a linear discriminant (Nilsson 1965, Section 2.12).

To keep the presentation in this report conceptually simple, assume that all d ϕ_j-functions are computed in the last stage of the receptor. If so, d and ϕ_j become equal to what has been (and will be) understood by p and Ξ_i, and Φ_i becomes a linear discriminant like $g_{i_L}(\Xi)$. Pattern classes which can be separated by a Φ-machine will in the following be called linearly separable.

1.7.3.5 The Nonlinear Generalized Discriminant. A different way of applying the concept of a discriminant function is to use only one function, the "Nonlinear Generalized Discriminant" (Sebestyen 1962, pp. 131-134), instead of using N_C discriminant functions. The nonlinear generalized discriminant is a function, $U = U(\Xi_1, \ldots, \Xi_p)$, which could be plotted in a (p+1)-dimensional space obtained by adding a U-axis to the decision space. The discriminant has the property that its value over all C_i-regions in decision space fall in one interval U_i on the U-axis, and that the N_C intervals on the U-axis, U_1, U_2. etc. do not overlap. Based on the U-value for an un-labeled pattern (or rather the U-interval in which it falls) it may con-sequently be decided to which of the N_C classes the pattern belongs. "In practice, however, the number of coefficients that must be determined in finding a suitable approximation of the nonlinear function becomes very large as the number of classes, dimensions of the space, and degree of the approximating function are raised. The matrix that must be inverted to find the optimum choice of unknown coefficients becomes prohibitively large. It is for this reason that less sophisticated methods must often be em-ployed to solve practical problems," (Sebestyen 1962, p. 133).

1.7.3.6 Parametric Training of Discriminants. Sometimes the designer makes decisions using the likelihood method, Subsection 1.6.4, or equi-valent procedures. In such cases the categorizer may be implemented by (i) a memory containing the N_C multivariate density functions and (ii) a comparator which selects the class for which membership is most likely given the Ξ-value of the unlabeled pattern. The N_C density functions are discriminants which must be determined by parametric training; they can be estimated by any of the methods described in Subsection 1.7.1.

A particular case with modest storage requirements deserves special mention. It is the case where the p attributes are all two-valued. The two values are called 1 and 0. Assume that attribute no. k, Ξ_k, takes the value 1 with probability $p_{k,j}$ for members of C_j, $j=1, 2, \ldots, N_C$. Let it be assumed that the attributes are statistically independent. Under the in-dependence assumption the multivariate density for members of C_j is $P_j(\Xi)$.

$$P_j(\Xi) = P_{pr}(j) \cdot \prod_{k=1}^{p} (p_{k,j}^{\Xi_k} \cdot (1-p_{k,j})^{1-\Xi_k}) \qquad ; (1.16)$$

$$\log(P_j(\Xi))=\log(P_{pr}(j))+\sum_{k=1}^{p}(\log(1-p_{k,j})+\Xi_k\cdot\log(p_{k,j}/(1-p_{k,j}))) \qquad ; (1.17)$$

$\log(P_j(\Xi))$ increases monotonically with $P_j(\Xi)$; the N_C functions, $\log(P(\Xi_j))$, $j=1$, ..., N_C can consequently be used as <u>linear</u> discriminants when the designer has knowledge of or can estimate the probabilities in Equation 1.17. Equation 1.17 shows that $\log(P_j(\Xi))$ is a linear function of Ξ_1, ..., Ξ_p; such a function is simple to implement with a summing circuit.

1.7.4 <u>Categorization of Members from More than Two Classes.</u> When the partitioning of pattern space is <u>implicit</u> as described in Subsection 1.7.3, the categorizer design is in principle the same for the cases $N_C = 2$ and $N_C>2$. The only difference between the two cases is that a larger categorizer may be needed when N_C increases; e.g., the stored representative points represent more classes if "nearest neighbor classification" (Article 1.7.3.1) is used, and the number of a posteriori probabilities (one per class) that must be computed and compared in a conditional probability computer (Selfridge 1959) will also increase. When the partitioning of the pattern space is <u>explicit</u> and $N_C = 2$, it is convenient to locate members of one class of patterns on the "inside" of the separation surface and the members of the other class on the "outside". With $N_C>2$ this simplicity is lost; the problem may, however, be solved by one of the following four methods for separation of N_C classes by use of hyperplanes. All four methods are based on the reduction of the N_C class problem to a set of two class problems.

Method no. 1. The N_C classes are separated pairwise (Highleyman 1962), this technique requires $N_C(N_C-1)/2$ or fewer hyperplanes. A pattern is considered a member of Class C_i when the corresponding point falls on the C_i-side of each of the (N_C-1) hyperplanes that separate members of C_i from members of the other (N_C-1) classes.

Method no. 2. As a first step it is only attempted to separate members of two of the N_C classes, say C_a and C_b. The resulting hyperplane will in all likelihood divide the representative members of one or more of the remaining (N_C-2) classes unevenly, say 90% vs. 10%. Let it be assumed that almost all of the members of C_c fell on the positive side of the hyperplane just like the members of C_a and almost all of the members of C_d fell on the negative side of the hyperplane where the members of class C_b are located. Furthermore, let it be assumed that the members of each of the remaining (N_C-4) classes were divided evenly by the hyperplane, 50% vs. 50%. In a next step it will be attempted to separate members of C_a and C_c from members of C_b and C_d. Assume that the attempt succeeds and that the members of the remaining (N_C-4) classes still tend to be divided evenly by the plane. If so, the result may be illustrated by a column in a truth table with two 1-digits for C_a and C_c, two 0-digits for C_b and C_d, and (N_C-4) don't-care-statements; such a column marked Hpl is shown in Table 1.1. By continuing this procedure a set of S_H hyperplanes may be found that determines a truth table with (S_H+1) columns and N_C rows. Any two rows should differ with respect to the 1- or 0-entries in at least one column. A decision regarding class membership of an unlabeled pattern may now be reached in the following manner. First it is determined on which side of

Hp 1	Hp 2	Hp 3	Hp 4	Class
1	1	0	d.c.	a
0	d.c.	1	0	b
1	0	d.c.	1	c
0	d.c.	0	1	d
d.c.	0	0	0	e
d.c.	1	1	1	f

Separation of the members of six classes by 4 hyperplanes.

Method no. 2, Subsection 1.7.4 is used. Hp 1 means hyperplane no. 1, etc.; d.c. illustrates the don't-care condition. As an example of the classification procedure consider a pattern that is located on the positive side of all four hyperplanes. The pattern is coded '1111' and is classified as being a member of Class f. A pattern with code '1010' would be rejected as not belonging to any of the six classes in question.

Table 1.1

each of the S_H hyperplanes the corresponding point is located. Location on the positive side is indicated by a logic 1, location on the plane or on the negative side is indicated by a logic 0. Secondly, by a suitable logic, the location of the point as expressed by a string of S_H binits is compared to the N_C rows and it is decided to which, if any, of the N_C classes the pattern belongs. A numerical example with $N_C = 6$ is presented in Table 1.1.

This second method requires fewer hyperplanes than the first method. The value of S_H is bounded by the following two expressions in N_C.

$$N_C(N_C-1)/2 \geqslant S_H \geqslant \log_2 (N_C) \qquad\qquad ; (1.18)$$

It should be realized that the second method requires some planning of the trial-and-error-procedure, whereas no such effort is needed with methods no. 1, 3 or 4.

Method no. 3. The N_C classes are separated by N_C hyperplanes. With this technique hyperplane no. i should be so located that it on one side has the members of Class C_i and on the other side the members of the other (N_C-1) classes. The method may be considered when the representative members of each class form a tight cluster and the $N_C(N_C-1)/2$ distances between clusters all are large compared to the largest "cluster-radius". In that case each of the N_C hyperplanes should be located so that it separates the N_C "points of finite size" in the manner just described. If the designer can implement hyperspheres or orthotopes (the p-dimensional equivalent of a 3-dimensional box), he may consider the possibility of locating the members of each class inside a particular closed surface. This form of categorizer has the particular advantage that the addition of a new class, Class no. N_C+1, only may require the addition of a new closed surface rather than a complete redesign of the categorizer (Bonner 1966). Method no. 4. Reformulation as a two-class problem. It is desired to find a set of N_C separation surfaces which can separate the pattern points representative of C_i, i=1, ..., N_C from the pattern points representative of the remaining (N_C-1) classes. It is known a priori that the representative pattern points from any two classes are linearly separable. It is possible to reduce this problem to a two class problem in a space with more than p dimensions by a reformulation. With this technique a set of N_C hyperplanes can always be located after a finite number of iterations (Duda and Hart 1973, Section 5.12). In the case where the N_C classes are not separable related techniques may be used (Wee and Fu 1968; Duda and Hart 1973, Table 5-1).

It has been shown in this subsection that the problem of separating members of N_C classes can be reduced to the problem of separating members of two classes. In the remaining part of this book it will be assumed, unless otherwise stated, that $N_C = 2$, so that only two pattern classes are of concern.

1.8 Hardware Implementation.

Besides constraints on funding and on time available for job completion, the designer must keep other limiting factors in mind during the receptor and categorizer design, especially if the design should be realized in hardware. The designer will usually want the operations in the PR to have the following two properties.

(1) A reliable and economical implementation of the operations should be possible. This means that certain esoteric functions may have to be ruled

out although they could have been used to measure the values of interesting attributes. Functions that can be realized with digital circuitry will usually be found to give promises of high reliability because such designs may be realized with integrated circuitry. There are certain applications where volume and weight are of more than usual concern, e.g., space- and medical electronics. In such areas schemes which at first may seem a bit far fetched, such as the parapropagation concept (Glucksman 1965), may become attractive on account of hardware that is made up of integrated circuit modules. The FOBW-technique that is described in the following chapters does also result in a potentially reliable hardware implementation as will be seen in Chapter 7. Often a PR will be located in a hostile environment because the integration of a sensor with a PR promises a substantial reduction in data handling. In such cases circuit design problems can be expected to influence the PR design. E.g., when the ambient temperature is high it becomes necessary to use design methods that will maximize the probability of not having the system fail due to drift failure or to catastrophic failure (Becker and Jensen 1974).

(2) The results should be available quickly and without use of excessive memory. How critical these requirements are changes from project to project. In many cases, however, the designer may find it to his advantage to use schemes where (i) the attribute values may be computed in parallel rather than in series and where (ii) the unlabeled pattern can be processed little by little as it is presented to the receptor (Bonner 1966), rather than after the complete pattern has been stored in a buffer memory. In Chapter 7 it will be shown that the FOBW technique requires only little memory: a shift-register to recall the immediate past of a binary sequence

with precision, and p counters of some kind (one per attribute) to generate the frequencies of occurrence of certain selected binary words; the contents of the counters give a statistical description of the more distant past of the binary sequence. The p binary word frequencies are generated in parallel and are quickly available for processing in the categorizer.

Building PRs by simulating the nervous system is potentially a very powerful approach. It seems, however, that substantial advances in the field of integrated circuitry are required before the full potential of the method can be realized. The requirement of a large-capacity memory may not be too serious (Hodges 1972; Feth 1973). The real stumblingblock seems to be the lack of a simple electronic equivalent of a neuron that can be massproduced in net-configurations. Also the modeling of neurons has been an active field. An important problem here is to obtain recoverable neuristor propagation (Kunow 1967; Parmentier 1970), the neuristor being the electronic equivalent of the nerve axon; the interested reader is referred to the Special Issue on "Studies of Neural Elements and Systems", Proceedings of the IEEE, June 1968.

The field of pattern recognition is rapidly expanding. The diversity of the field - stimulating as it is - also presents problems. Any author in the field is forced more or less to ignore important topics; e.g., we have not mentioned such areas as Scene Analysis (Duda and Hart 1973, Part II) and Syntactic Methods (Fu 1974).

The reader who wants to keep up with the vigorous growth of the pattern recognition field is advised to read the publications mentioned in the Bibliography. A new and most valuable contribution to the literature is the Proceedings from the bi-annual International Joint Conference on Pattern Recognition; e.g., the invited survey papers in SIJCPR 1974 give an excellent exposition of the state of the art.

2.   DESIGN OF A PATTERN RECOGNIZER USING THE
FREQUENCY OF OCCURRENCE OF BINARY WORDS METHOD

2.1 Introduction.

In this chapter a technique is described for the design of devices
which automatically can classify patterns, assuming that the patterns
can be coded as long binary sequences. The described technique is called
the "Frequency of Occurrence of Binary Words" technique or the FOBW
technique. The FOBW technique has two interesting features.

(1) The final design is amenable to microminiaturization. This is a
distinct advantage in many medical and space applications because it
opens possibilities for integration of the sensor that generates the
pattern with the PR. When the PR is added to the sensor, only the PR output, rather than the sensor output, will have to be sent to the central
processor. This usually will result in a substantial reduction of the
total data flow. The hardware realization of a PR designed with the FOBW
technique will be discussed further in Chapter 7.

(2) The FOBW technique presents one possible answer to an important,
unsolved problem in the area of pattern recognition. The problem arises
in the following manner. The designer has discovered a number of attributes, all of which are to some limited extent effective in his classification efforts. The number of such attributes is substantially larger
than N_H where N_H is the largest number of attributes that can be imple-

mented in the final hardware or software realization of the PR. The problem may be stated as follows: how should the designer use the many not too effective attributes to generate N_H more effective attributes? Can the designer by some procedure "breed" a new generation of more effective attributes? The FOBW technique proposes an answer to this problem when the patterns can be coded as long binary sequences. The answer utilizes the fact that shorter binary words can be combined to give longer binary words.

The problem areas where the FOBW technique in particular can be useful are those where the patterns are long and noisy, without too well defined beginnings and ends, and where the patterns in a meaningful manner can be coded as binary sequences. In such situations attributes of a statistical nature such as the observed frequency of occurrence of certain selected binary words seem to be appropriate. The FOBW method can, however, be used with almost any kind of patterns. To make the following description simple, only waveform patterns will be considered. Notice that a two-dimensional pattern may be given a waveform description by suitable scanning, e.g. by plotting the amplitude along a spacefilling curve (Abend et al. 1965, Section 6). The waveform patterns which the PR should be able to classify are typically generated by some physical, bio-logical, or physiological process. The binary word frequencies of occurrence will in the following for the sake of brevity also be referred to as "frequencies". The frequencies are the only kind of pattern attributes discussed in the remaining part of this report; the frequencies can, of course, be used side by side with other more conventional attributes if the designer believes that such a receptor will be effective.

2.2 A Step by Step Description of the FOBW Design Procedure.

The diagram in Figure 2.1 illustrates the nine steps in the design of a PR when the FOBW method is used. It is assumed in this section that a pattern always belongs to one of two classes, Class A or Class B; this assumption is not very restrictive for the reasons given in Subsection 1.7.4. Classes A and B are equivalent to C_1 and C_2 from Chapter 1.

(1) First the designer will contact the specialists in the field, as indicated by Block no. 1, Figure 2.1. The designer wants to learn how in the opinion of the specialists (i) the process or processes that generate the patterns may be modeled (Block no. 5) and how (ii) a library of representative waveforms should be obtained (Block no. 3). The data collection phase (Block no. 3) is often expensive and demanding in time and funding. It is crucial that the greatest care be exercised during this phase because the future PR is designed by generalizing from these recorded members of Classes A and B. Quite often in practice, however, the library of waveforms has already been obtained so the recording methods are beyond the control of the designer. Block no. 4 illustrates a study of the waveform records by the designer. The study is not intended to be a painstaking effort, its purpose is to insure that more obvious waveform characteristics are detected and incorporated in the process model. The study begins with a visual inspection of the representative waveforms. Next some simpler parameters, e.g. the waveform mean (Fine and Johnson 1965; Anderson 1965) may be studied for each waveform. Then the waveforms are tested for hunches regarding their nature. E.g. the hypothesis that a waveform has been generated by a Gaussian process may be tested by the Chi-Squared method. It should be noticed that when a statistical method is selected for testing a hypothesis,

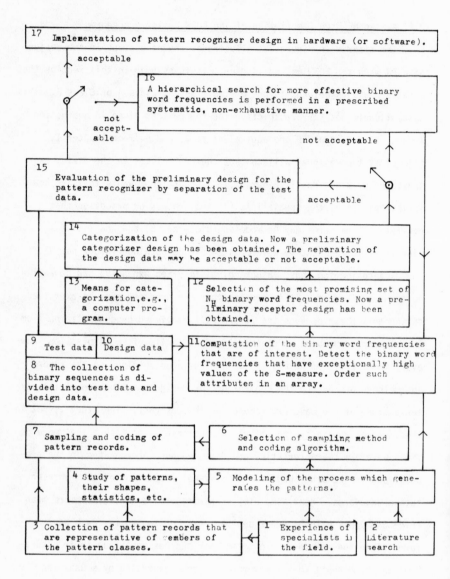

17 Implementation of pattern recognizer design in hardware (or software).

↑ acceptable

16 A hierarchical search for more effective binary word frequencies is performed in a prescribed systematic, non-exhaustive manner.

not acceptable

not acceptable

15 Evaluation of the preliminary design for the pattern recognizer by separation of the test data.

acceptable

14 Categorization of the design data. Now a preliminary categorizer design has been obtained. The separation of the design data may be acceptable or not acceptable.

13 Means for categorization, e.g., a computer program.

12 Selection of the most promising set of N_H binary word frequencies. Now a preliminary receptor design has been obtained.

9 Test data **10** Design data

8 The collection of binary sequences is divided into test data and design data.

11 Computation of the binary word frequencies that are of interest. Detect the binary word frequencies that have exceptionally high values of the S-measure. Order such attributes in an array.

7 Sampling and coding of pattern records.

6 Selection of sampling method and coding algorithm.

4 Study of patterns, their shapes, statistics, etc.

5 Modeling of the process which generates the patterns.

3 Collection of pattern records that are representative of members of the pattern classes.

1 Experience of specialists in the field.

2 Literature search

Graphical description of the design of a pattern recognizer with the FOBW method.

Figure 2.1

(Lehman 1959), the method should be chosen in the light of what is
known about the distribution of the variables and the number of samples
available. If no information is available about the distribution, the
designer must use a non-parametric or rank test (Siegel 1956; Carlyle
and Thomas 1964; Hájek and Sidak 1967). E.g. the hypothesis that the
distribution of amplitude values is stationary can be tested with a Wald-
Wolfowitz runs test (Siegel 1956, Chapter 6). Block no. 2 illustrates a
search through the pertinent literature by a librarian. Such a search is
inexpensive and will often be found to give excellent returns. Based on
the information from Blocks no. 1, 2 and 4 the designer decides on a
model for the kind of process or processes that generated the Class A and
Class B waveforms. The modeling problem has been discussed in the literature (Martin 1968) and will be discussed further in Chapter 5. The essen-
tial thing about the process model is that it is completely described by
certain parameters ϕ_1, ϕ_2, ..., etc., and that the set of parameters
usually has different values for each of the pattern records in the
library of representative patterns. The features that are believed to
separate members of Class A from members of Class B should, of course,
be related to the process model parameters.

(2) When a model has been generated in Block no. 5 the designer is faced
with the problem of selecting a sampling method and a binary coding algorithm for the waveform patterns. Work with this problem is illustrated
by Block no. 6. The algorithm must have the property that the interesting
model parameters give rise to attributes in the form of frequencies of
occurrence of certain binary words in the coded waveform. It is not
necessary to know the precise nature of this mapping of process parameter values into binary word frequencies as long as there is assurance

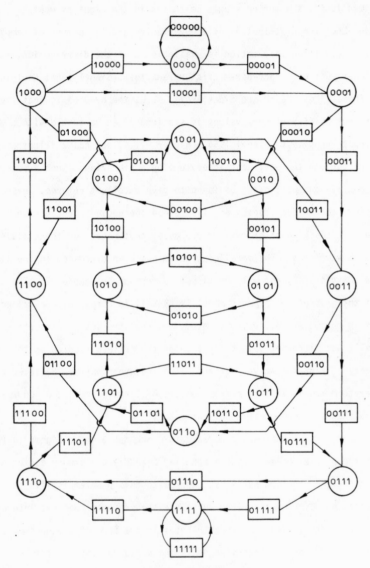

Flow diagram.
Figure 2.2

that for each record the actual values of the separating features largely have been preserved in some form in the values of the binary word frequencies for the coded record. There is no guarantee that, a sampling and
coding algorithm can always be found. In Chapter 5 some examples of algorithms will be given that can be used in a large number of cases. A
typical algorithm is the "sign algorithm": sample the waveform at some
specified constant rate, code all positive samples as '1' and all non-
positive samples as '0'.

The representative patterns are all sampled and coded as indicated
by Block no. 7. This step is usually tantamount to a substantial data
reduction. From hereon the work proceeds with a library of representative binary sequences. A sequence may consist of just a few binits; in
most practical cases, however, each sequence will consist of many
thousands of binits.

(3) The library of binary sequences is divided into two groups for
reasons discussed in Subsection 1.4.2. The first group, the Design Data,
is used to obtain a preliminary design for the PR. The group contains
M_{AD} members of Class A and M_{BD} members of Class B. Only this group will
be considered in Steps no. 4 through 8 in this section. The second group
of binary sequences, the Test Data, is used in a later, computer simulated test of the designed machine. The test data group contains M_{AT}
members of Class A and M_{BT} members of Class B. The division of the data
is indicated by Blocks no. 8, 9 and 10.

(4) The N-grams constitute an important class of binary words. First an
example is given of how the N-gram frequencies of occurrence are determined. Consider the binary sequence '11111000000' which contains 11
binits. The sequence could also be said to contain 10 pairs of adjacent

binits. Each pair of adjacent binits is called a Digram. The "frequency of occurrence" for each of the four digrams in the sequence is $f_{11}=4/10$, $f_{10}=1/10$, $f_{01}=0/10$, and $f_{00}=5/10$.

Any binary sequence has a one to one correspondence with a path through a flow diagram like the diagram illustrated in Figure 2.2. The diagram is drawn for the case with 4 and 5 binit words called Tetragrams and Pentagrams. Similar diagrams may be drawn for any set of N-grams and (N+1)-grams; the simple case with N=4 will now be used to illustrate the concept of f_ψ. On the figure each of the 16 possible Tetragrams is indicated by a circle and each of the possible Pentagrams is indicated by a rectangle. If a logic '1' or a '0' is added on the right side of a four binit binary word Ψ, the five binit word $\Psi 1$ or $\Psi 0$ is obtained. The two possibilities are indicated by arrows on the two lines that connect each circle with two rectangles. When the leftmost digit in a five binit word is discarded, a four binit word is obtained. This operation is indicated by an arrow on the line that connects each rectangle with a circle. Let the four leftmost digits in a binary sequence from the library of representative sequences be called Ψ. Ψ is illustrated by one of the 16 circles; the circle constitutes the beginning of a path through the flow-diagram. By alternatingly adding the next digit in the sequence on the right side of the four binit word and discarding the leftmost digit in the resulting five binit word a path may be traced through the flow-diagram. The number of times the path touches the Ψ circle divided by the number of times it touches any of the 16 circles, is by definition equal to the frequency of occurrence of the tetragram Ψ, f_ψ. The sum of the 16 tetragram frequencies is unity. For values of N other than 4 the sum of the 2^N N-gram frequencies is also

16 Tetragrams		8 Trigrams		4 Digrams		2 Symbols	
'1111'	5	'111'	7	'11'	10	'1'	13
'1110'	2	'110'	2				
'1101'	0	'101'	0	'10'	2		
'1100'	2	'100'	2				
'1011'	0	'011'	2	'01'	2	'0'	19
'1010'	0	'010'	0				
'1001'	0	'001'	2	'00'	17		
'1000'	2	'000'	15				
'0111'	1						
'0110'	0						
'0101'	0						
'0100'	0						
'0011'	2						
'0010'	0						
'0001'	2						
'0000'	13						
	29		30		31		32

N-gram frequencies of occurrence computed for the 32 binit sequence:
11111000111110000000000000000011

Table 2.1

M, the separation (in sampling intervals) of symbols in digram

Delayed digram	1	2	3	4	5	6	7	8	9	10	11	12	13
'1-M-1'	10	7	5	4	3	3	4	5	5	4	3	2	1
'1-M-0'	2	4	6	7	8	8	7	6	6	7	8	9	10
'0-M-1'	2	4	5	5	5	4	3	2	2	2	2	2	2
'0-M-0'	17	15	13	12	11	11	11	11	10	9	8	7	6
	—	—	—	—	—	—	—	—	—	—	—	—	—
	31	30	29	28	27	26	25	24	23	22	21	20	19

Delayed digram frequencies of occurrence computed for the 32 binit sequence:
11111000111110000000000000011

Table 2.2

unity.

Each of the $M_{AD} + M_{BD}$ binary sequences is scanned to determine the frequencies of occurrence of the 2 Symbols '1' and '0', the 4 Digrams '11', '10', '01', and '00', the 8 Trigrams meaning three binit binary words, the Tetragrams, the Pentagrams, the Hexagrams, the Heptagrams, the Octagrams, etc. Usually it is only practical to measure all N-gram frequencies, where N is less than seven or eight.

There are, as may be expected certain algebraic relationships between the N-gram frequencies. Such relationships will be discussed in Chapter 3; they are influenced by the length of the binary sequences.

Each of the $M_{AD}+M_{BD}$ binary sequences in the design data group has by now been described by two Symbol frequencies f_0 and f_1, four Digram frequencies f_{00}, f_{01}, f_{10}, and f_{11}, eight Trigram frequencies f_{000}, f_{001}, etc. up to 2^N N-gram frequencies of occurrence.

Table 2.1 lists the N-gram frequencies for a (very short) sequence consisting of 32 binits.

(5) The digrams with delays constitute a different class of binary words. Each binary sequence is scanned to determine the frequencies of occurrence of digrams with delays, also called Di-delay-grams. The di-delay-gram '1-M-0' for instance, is present in a binary sequence whenever a '1' after a separation of M sampling intervals (or M-1 binits) is followed by a '0'; e.g., '1-4-0 is present once in the 5 binit sequence '10110'. A delayed digram '1-M-0' could be said to be an (M+1)-gram with "don't care" states for all but the first and the last binit. For M=1 the di-delay-gram becomes an ordinary digram as mentioned in Step 4; the one sampling interval which separates the binits is not indicated in this case to avoid confusion with the logic '1' sign. For M=0 the di-delay-

gram frequencies f_{1-M-1}, f_{1-M-0}, f_{0-M-1}, and f_{0-M-0} degenerate into f_1, 0, 0, and f_0.

Di-delay-gram frequencies with a range of delays, 2 to M_{max} sampling intervals are computed for each sequence using some suitable increment. The delays could typically have the values 2, 4, 6, 8, 10, etc. sampling intervals. The algebraic relationships between delayed digram frequencies will be discussed in Chapter 3. Each binary sequence in the design data group by now has been described also by 4 frequencies of occurrence for each delay M of the di-delay-grams. Table 2.2 lists the delayed digram frequencies for the (very short) binit sequence consisting of 32 binits.

(6) The result of Steps no 4 and 5 is that each of the M_{AD} plus M_{BD} binary sequences has been described in a statistical sense by (usually several hundred) attributes each of which is the frequency of occurrence of a particular binary word. Step no. 4 and 5 usually result in a sub-stantial data reduction. The two steps are illustrated by Block no. 11. The M_{AD} plus M_{BD} sets of attribute values constitute the starting point for a search for a set of N_H (or fewer) attributes that will give adequate separation of the Class A and Class B members. N_H is the largest number of different pattern attributes the designer can afford to implement. Typically, N_H is between 5 and 150. The search for an effective set of N_H attributes is tantamount to a design of the PR by iteration as will become apparent during the remaining part of this section.

For each attribute the value of a suitable measure of separability, MS, is computed. The value is an estimate of the ability of the attribute, when used alone, to separate members of Class A from members of Class B. Seven possible MS functions were listed in Subsection 1.5.4, any of which will do. In Sections 2.3 and 4.2 some reasons are given why the

S-measure may be regarded as particularly useful. In the following it is
assumed that the S-measure is used. Next the attributes are ordered in an
array according to their value of the MS. The ordering of the attributes
will be described further in Section 2.3. The array is the main design
variable. After the array has been established all the coming events in
the PR design effort have largely been determined. The designer selects
N_H attributes from the top of the ordered array. The selection of the N_H
frequencies is a first preliminary receptor design as indicated by Block
no. 12 in Figure 2.1.

(7) Any binary sequence from the library of representative sequences may
be described by a point in N_H-dimensional space which as coordinates have
the values of the N_H attributes. The M_{AD} points representing the design
data members of Class A plus the M_{AB} points representing the members of
Class B constitute the input for the means for categorization by which
the preliminary categorizer is designed. Block no. 13 indicates the means
for categorization; the topic of categorization was discussed in Section
1.7. The means for categorization is usually a computer program plus
computer, the means could also be a trainable device (Block 1962; Brain
et el. 1963; Widrow et el. 1963; Steinbuch and Piske 1963). The result of
the categorizer design is in geometrical terms the location of a separation surface of given functional form, e.g. a hyperplane. The surface
separates the representative Class A points from the representative
Class B points in an optimum manner according to the selected decision
procedure. Four possible decision procedures were described in Section
1.6. Usually some of the points will be misclassified. During the categorization procedure it should be noticed which attributes seem to contribute most to the separation. This important point was discussed in

Subsection 1.5.6, and it will be discussed further in Section 2.5.

The computation of a preliminary categorizer constitutes step no. 7 in the FOBW design procedure. When the categorizer has been computed, a preliminary design for the pattern recognizer has been obtained. It consists of the preliminary receptor followed by the preliminary categorizer. Step no. 7 is illustrated by Block no. 14.

The preliminary design may be considered "not acceptable" for several reasons, the most common reason being that too many of the M_{AD} plus M_{BD} members of the design data group were misclassified by the categorizer. If so, new and better attributes, meaning frequencies of occurrence of new binary words, are needed. The way in which new and promising attributes are generated is an important feature of the FOBW method. The feature is illustrated by Block no. 16 and will be discussed in Chapter 6. Basically the idea is the following: let ψ_{11}, ψ_{12}, etc. be binary words, the frequencies of which, $f_{\psi_{11}}$, $f_{\psi_{12}}$, etc. seemed to contribute most to the separation in the first attempt; we now create a second generation of new and longer binary words ψ_{21}, ψ_{22}, etc. which contain the shorter words ψ_{11}, ψ_{12}, etc; e.g., '111001' contains '11100' and '11001'. It will be demonstrated in Chapter 6 that it is "quite likely" that $f_{\psi_{21}}$, $f_{\psi_{22}}$, etc. are better attributes than $f_{\psi_{11}}$, $f_{\psi_{12}}$, etc.

The frequencies of occurrence of the new and promising binary words are computed for each of the M_{AD} plus M_{BD} binary sequences in Block no. 11. Next the value of the S-measure is computed for each new attribute. The S-values give an estimate of the separating capability for each of the new and promising attributes; the higher the S-value the better the attribute is assumed to be. From the highest valued of the new attributes and, if necessary, the attributes which by now are at the top of the array, a new set of N_H attributes is obtained. The new set of attributes is equivalent to a new preliminary receptor design as indicated by Block no. 12. The generation of new attribute sets will be discussed in more detail in Section 2.4.

Each time a new set of N_H more promising attributes has been selected, the new and presumably more effective receptor is tried out; Step no. 7 is repeated. Som of the second, third, fourth, etc. generation attributes may be of a new type: the frequency of occurrence of short N-grams with delays of more than one sampling interval between some of the adjacent binits. The new attributes are called Delayed N-grams. E.g., the Delayed Trigram $f_{1-D-0-E-0}$ is the frequency of occurrence of the binary word 1-D-0-E-0: a logic '1' followed D sampling intervals later by a logic '0' which in turn is followed E intervals later by a logic '0'; either D, E or both should be more than unity.

When the preliminary PR design separates the design data in an "acceptable"manner, step no. 8 has been accomplished; this usually requires some iterations. The number of attributes used in the design is called p as in Figure 1.1, $p \leq N_H$. In most practical cases $p=N_H$. $p<N_H$ occurs in the rare cases where perfect categorization is achieved with fewer than N_H attributes; the possibility is discussed in Section 2.4. Step no. 8 is carried out by the feedback loop of Blocks no. 16, 11, 12, and 14.

(9) How well can the latest preliminary pattern recognizer, consisting of the preliminary receptor followed by the preliminary categorizer, be expected to perform? This problem was discussed in Subsection 1.4.2. An estimate of the error probability may be obtained by letting the preliminary pattern recognizer separate the Class A and Class B binary sequences

from the test data group (Highleyman 1962a). The estimate is obtained by
taking the following steps. First, the values of the p frequencies of
occurrence of binary words that were used as attributes in the latest of
the preliminary receptor designs are computed for each of the M_{AT} plus
M_{BT} binary sequences. Each of the test data sequences may now be described
by a point in p-dimensional space. Secondly, the average cost of classification of the test data is computed, if the designer has used Bayes'
procedure; if the designer has used a different decision procedure, the
corresponding index of performance is computed. The result may be taken
as an estimate of the quality of the PR design. Also, the confidence
limits for the estimate should be computed, if possible, (Highleyman
1962a). If the preliminary PR design is acceptable, the design is considered final, and the PR is realized in hardware (or software). If the
preliminary design is not acceptable, the PR design is modified by iteration so that it can separate the design data, with even greater accuracy.
The modified PR design is again used in Block no. 15 to separate the test
data. If the separation by now is acceptable, the PR design is realized in
hardware. If the separation of the test data is still found "not acceptable"
the PR is again modified by iteration so that it can separate the design
data even better, etc. The underlying assumption is that the series of PR
designs which separate the design data more and more accurately presumably
also will separate the test data more and more accurately. If it becomes
apparent that the test data cannot be separated sufficiently well by a
continuation of the iteration procedure, this first effort has failed.
The many decisions, which were made before the first design effort began,
will have to be re-evaluated, and questions of the following soul-
searching kind will have to be answered. Precisely what makes us think

that members of Class A can be separated from members of Class B? Are
the recorded data representative, and do they really contain the patterns
in question? Is the separation surface of a suitable functional form or
should some other form be used? Nothing is more valuable than a good
hunch; have any hunches been overlooked, which could have been helpful
in the modeling (Block no. 5) and in the selection of the sampling method
and coding algorithm (Block no. 6)? Depending on the answers to such
questions it may be decided to start all over from Step no. 1 or to consider the problem as being unsolvable with the state of the art.

2.3 The Ordered Array of Attributes.

In Section 2.2, Step no. 6, it was mentioned how the designer
estimates the separating ability of each attribute by computing the value
of a suitable measure of separability. Seven possible functions were
listed in Subsection 1.5.4 so the question may be asked: what makes one
MS better than another MS? In practice it is important that the multivariate distributions of Class A patterns as well as Class B patterns
both be simple functions, preferably unimodal, and at least not disjointed so that the two classes may be separated by a separation surface
of simple form; this matter was discussed in Subsection 1.7.2. Each
attribute should therefore be evaluated by a MS having the following
three properties. (1) The MS should indicate the extent to which the two
distributions do overlap. (2) The MS should penalize multimodal and
especially essentially disjointed distributions like those in Figure 1.3.
The reason for this is the assumption that multivariate Class A and
Class B distributions, which have p marginal unimodal distributions
(like those illustrated in Figure 1.2) rather than marginal multimodal

distributions (like those illustrated in Figure 1.3), tend to be unimodal. If the p attributes have unimodal distributions and are statistically independent, the multivariate distributions will be unimodal;
if the independence assumption is not satisfied, the multivariate
distributions may on occation be multimodal (Papoulis 1965, Figure 6-19).
(3) The MS should be simple to compute timewise and computer-memory-
wise.

All seven measures listed in Subsection 1.5.3 have the first property,
but only the last two, the Fisher-measure and the S-measure, have the
second property as an inspection of Figures 1.2 and 1.3 will reveal. The
two measures do not make use of the complete Class A and Class B sample
densities. They only make use of the first two moments of each density
and in a computationally simple manner. The four moments can be computed by memory saving recursion formulas, consequently, the Fisher
measure and the S-measure have the third property to a higher degree
than the first five measures. In Section 4.2 some reasons are given
why the S-measure may be preferred to the other six measures. Unless
otherwise indicated, it is assumed that the S-measure is used.

When the designer has computed the value of the S-measure for each
attribute, he will order the attributes according to decreasing values
and discard attributes with very low values. An example of an array consisting of six attributes is f_{110}, f_{0-2-1}, f_{1-17-0}, f_{0-7-0}, f_{011}. In
practice an array will typically consist of several hundred attributes.

2.4 The Generation of New Sets of N_H Attributes.

In the last part of Step no. 6, Section 2.2, it was described how
the designer selects the first set of N_H attributes. He takes the

attributes from the top of the aray one by one. Each time a design has been found "not acceptable" the designer is faced with the problem of generating a new set of attributes. The designer will proceed in the following manner. First he examines the latest categorization of the design data in detail to find out which of the N_H attributes seemed to be most effective in the separation. How credit with some confidence may be assigned to the individual attributes was discussed in Subsection 1.5.6 and will be discussed further in Section 2.5. Assume that the designer found N_E attributes which according to some criterion were effective in the categorization effort, $N_E < N_H$. The designer will then discard the remaining $(N_H - N_E)$ attributes. The designer can generate a new attribute set with N_H members in two different ways.

(1) The designer can bypass Blocks no. 16 and 11, and go directly to Block no. 12 where he takes $(N_H - N_E)$ attributes from what is now the top of the array. The new set of N_H attributes is obtained by adding the $(N_H - N_E)$ attributes to the N_E attributes which showed effectiveness in the previous categorization attempt. This procedure is an inexpensive way in which to generate a new attribute set in the sense that the designer only makes use of the information already present in the ordered array of attributes. The possibilities with this approach are limited by the finite numbers of attributes in the array. Also the best the designer can hope for is to find the most effective set of N_H attributes selected from the attributes in the array. With this method the designer does not attempt to generate new effective attributes.

(2)   The designer can, based on the N_E effective attributes in Block no. 16, make educated guesses (by methods described in Chapter 6) about new and longer binary words, the frequencies of which may have a good chance of being even better attributes than the N_E attributes; by better attributes are understood attributes that have higher values of the S-measure.   In Block no. 11 the actual S-values are computed for the suggested new attributes.   Those promising, new attributes that live up to expectations by having higher S-values than their "parent-attributes" are selected for the new attribute set and the parent attributes are discarded.   Those promising new attributes that do not have higher S-values than their "parent-attributes" are discarded and the "parent-attributes" are retained.   If the number of new attributes plus the number of retained "parent-attributes" is less than N_H, the necessary additional attributes are taken from what is now the top of the array.   This approach has much potential because the hierachies where the search takes place for the next generation of attributes are virtually unlimited in size; the designer can make his binary words longer and longer without much fear of running into implementation problems.   It should be noticed that with this second method (and contrary to the first method) it is neces-sary to scan all the M_{AD} plus M_{BD} sequences once in Block no. 11 during each iteration to compute the values of the new frequencies and to com-pute the S-values.

2.5   Detection of Effective Attributes.

In Block no. 14, Figure 2.1, the preliminary categorizer design is performed with the selected means for categorization.   The result of the categorizer design is equivalent to establishing the location of a decision surface of given functional form in such a way that the surface separates the Class A and Class B points in pattern space in an optimum manner according to some criterion, usually Bayes' criterion. Let the pattern space be p-dimensional and let, as in Figure 1.1, the p binary word frequencies be called Ξ_1, ..., Ξ_p. The question may now be asked: which of the attributes contribute most to the separation of Class A and Class B members? Three answers to this problem were given in Subsection 1.5.6. A fourth answer which is well suited for the FOBW design technique will now be described.

The following categorization procedure has been developed by Akers (Akers 1965). In the form of a computer program the procedure can serve as the means for categorization, Block 13 in Figure 2.1. With this procedure separation of the Class A and Class B points by a hyperplane is attempted using a pattern-space with a dimensionality that is as low, or almost as low as possible. An important by-product of the categorization is that attributes may be detected that have little or no incremental effectiveness; a discussion of effectiveness was presented in Subsection 1.5.3. In this manner the Akers-procedure gives a crude answer to the question posed at the end of the previous paragraph. The procedure is as follows. First separation is attempted in a one-dimensional space (using only one of the p-attributes). The M_{AD} plus M_{BD} points are read in one by one and located in the one-dimensional space. The one-dimensional hyperplane, a point, is continually adjusted to give 100% correct separation. Assume that a point, say P_{17}, cannot be classified correctly. The program will then examine the remaining (p-1) attributes to see if the introduction of a second attribute (meaning the addition of a dimension to pattern space) will make 100% correct separation possible for P_{17} plus the points which previously had been read in. This will usually be the case. If so, more points are read in, and the two dimensional hyperplane, a straight line, is continually adjusted to give 100% correct separation. Assume that a point, say P_{57}, cannot be classified correctly. The program will then examine the remaining (p-2) attributes to see if the introduction of a third attribute (meaning the addition of a dimension to pattern space) will make 100% correct separation possible for P_{57} plus the points which previously had been read in. In this manner, the program introduces dimension after dimension when needed. If the Class A and Class B points are linearly separable the program will find a separation plane that utilizes few (though not necessarily the minimum number of) attributes. If the Class A and Class B points are not linearly separable in p-dimension, the program will switch to a second mode. Now all points are read in, and an attempt is made to locate the hyperplane in such a manner that the number of misclassified point is made as small as possible. In this second mode, all p attributes are used.

In most practical cases it becomes necessary to use the second mode in the Akers program. When the second mode is used it should be noticed which attributes are introduced last. Such attributes, on the average, may be assumed to be less effective than the attributes used earlier. Usually the attributes used last are discarded. In this manner some insurance is obtained against having to implement a categorizer with ineffective attributes.

3. COMPUTATIONAL RULES FOR BINARY WORD FREQUENCIES OF OCCURRENCE

3.1 Binary Word Probabilities, Frequencies of Occurrence and Sequence
Length.

In this chapter it is assumed that each of the pattern records is
time stationary and that a record after sampling and coding constitutes
"an adequately long" binary sequence. By "adequately long" is understood
a length that permits the computation of each of the interesting binary
word frequencies to take place with the desired computational accuracy.

To define "adequate length" in a more formal manner it becomes necessary to consider an idealized, experimental situation where a stationary
process is capable of generating a binary sequence of unlimited length.
In this section Ψ indicates one particular (but arbitrary) N-gram and for
the present only frequencies of occurrence of N-grams of the same length
as Ψ are considered. If the binary sequence is periodic, a segment corresponding to one period will be of adequate length. When the process is
stochastic, the question of adequate length has to do with the estimation
of a probability with a desired confidence interval; this point will be
explained in the remaining part of this section where only stationary
stochastic processes are considered.

N adjacent binits anywhere in a sequence generated by the process
constitute an N-gram; let the probability that the N-gram is Ψ be p_Ψ.
To describe the sequence the designer must estimate p_Ψ. With estimates are

associated confidence intervals and only if each estimate is obtained with a suitable narrow confidence interval for each member of each pattern class can an acceptable PR be designed. The "adequate length" which is needed to obtain an estimate with a desired confidence interval may be determined in the following manner. A segment $L=L_1$ binits long of a binary sequence generated by the process is scanned and with suitable intervals the values of N adjacent binits are recorded; the intervals should be so long that the N-grams may be assumed to be <u>uncorrelated</u>. Each time an N-gram is recorded it is determined if it is of the form Ψ or if it is one of the other (2^N-1) possible N-grams of the form "not-Ψ". Let the total number of recorded N-grams be $\Gamma = \Gamma_1$ out of which $\gamma=\gamma_1$ have the form Ψ; γ_1/Γ_1 then becomes a consistent estimator for p_ψ. It may be demonstrated (Davenport and Root 1958, Art. 5-5) that γ_1/Γ_1 has the expected value p_ψ and the variance:

$$\sigma^2(\gamma_1/\Gamma_1) = p_\psi(1-p_\psi)/\Gamma_1 \qquad\qquad ; (3.1)$$

The maximum value of the variance is $1/(4\Gamma_1)$. When the results are substituted into the Tchebycheff inequality the following expression is obtained.

$$P(|\gamma_1/\Gamma_1-p_\psi|\geq\epsilon)\leq p_\psi(1-p_\psi)/(\Gamma_1\epsilon^2) \qquad\qquad ; (3.2)$$

The right hand side of the inequality is less than or equal to $1/(4\Gamma_1\epsilon^2)$ and may for small values of p_ψ be approximated by $p_\psi/(\Gamma_1\epsilon^2)$. Equation 3.1 shows that the variance of γ_1/Γ_1 tends to zero as the segment length, L_1 binits, and thereby the number of recorded N-grams increase without limit. According to the Bernoulli theorem γ_1/Γ_1 converges in probability

(Davenport and Root 1958, Art. 4-6; Papoulis 1965, Sec. 8-5) to p_ψ as the number Γ_1 of uncorrelated N-grams increases without limit.

A numerical example may illustrate how the designer decides if the segment consisting of L_1 binits is of adequate length for the estimation of p_ψ. Assume that the designer after counting uncorrelated N-grams finds that $\gamma_1 = 1000$, $\Gamma_1 = 4000$, and that he wants a 95% confidence interval of width $2\epsilon = 0.062$ for the estimate of p_ψ . The expected value for p_ψ is $\gamma_1/\Gamma_2 = 0.25$; the expected value is used instead of the unknown p_ψ on the right hand side of the Inequality 3.2. The numerical values are substituted into Inequality 3.2; with the assumed values it so happens that the inequality is satisfied.

$$P(\,|\gamma_1/\Gamma_1 - p_\psi|\, \geq\, \epsilon) \leq 0.25(1 - 0.25)/4000{\cdot}0.031^2) = 1 - 0.95 \; ; \qquad (3.3)$$

The segment is consequently of adequate length. Also, the estimate γ_1/Γ_1 of p_ψ is adequate for the chosen confidence interval. The estimate γ_1/Γ_1 is called f_ψ and used as described in Section 2.2. If the segment with L_1 binits was too short the computations are repeated for a longer segment consisting of L_2 binits containing Γ_2 uncorrelated N-grams, γ_2 of which are of the form ψ. If the second attempt is successful γ_2/Γ_2 is used as f_ψ. If the second attempt is unsuccessful a third attempt is made with an even longer segment consisting of L_3 binits, etc.

When the values of the N-grams are not only uncorrelated but also statistically independent (Davenport and Root 1958, Art. 5-5) the record of N-grams of the forms ψ and "not-ψ" form a Bernoulli trial. The probability distribution for γ_1/Γ_1 consequently becomes binomial, and for large values of Γ_1 the binomial distribution will tend to the Gaussian distribution, (Hald 1962, Sec. 21.5). Due to the known form of the distribution fewer

N-grams are needed to estimate p_ψ with a specified confidence interval

than when the Tchebycheff inequality is used. The confidence intervals

associated with different values of p_ψ are available in graphical form or

may be obtained from tables (Siegel 1956, pp. 36-42). It is interesting to

observe that when the distribution of γ_1/Γ_1 is known to be binomial a sub-

stantial reduction in adequate length results; e.g., when Γ_1 = 1000 and γ_1

= 250 (corresponding to 1/4 of the segment used before) it is seen

(Highleyman 1962 a, Figure 1) that p_ψ as before will fall in a 95% con-

fidence interval of width 2ϵ = 0.06, this time extending from 0.225 to

0.285.

Up until now only N-grams have been discussed. The material in the

section does, however, apply to frequencies of all types of binary words

because such words may be considered as N-grams where some of the binits

are in "don't care" states.

In many practical situations all the sampled and coded members of

Classes A and B will have less than adequate length. Even in such situa-

tions it may still be possible to estimate the probability density functions

$f_A(f_\psi)$ and $f_B(f_\psi)$ quite accurately for any frequency f_ψ as long as there

are sufficiently many members M_{AD} and M_{BD} of classes A and B. The question

of estimating density functions when only noisy measurements are available

has been discussed in the literature (Chien and Fu 1967; Wagner 1968).

In many cases the patterns are not stationary, contrary to the assump-

tion made above. Yet, in such situations the binary word frequencies may

still be effective pattern attributes. E.g., if the values of the para-

meters for the processes that generated the patterns (and through them the

instantaneous binary word frequencies) change with time in a well defined

manner, each observed binary word frequency constitutes a time-average that

very well could be an effective attribute.

As stated in the beginning of this section: in this chapter it is assumed that all binary sequences are stationary and of adequate length unless the opposite is indicated.

3.2 Redundant Information in N-Gram Frequencies.

3.2.1 The Problem. When the frequencies of occurrence of the 2^N possible N-grams are considered, the question may be asked: how many pieces of information are needed to compute the 2^N N-gram frequencies? An answer to this question is of theoretical interest and of value for the planning of the computational work.

In this section, Section 3.2, it will be demonstrated that the 2^N frequencies of occurrence of the N-grams in an "adequately long" binary sequence may be computed from the 2^{N-1} pieces of information: f_0, f_{00}, plus the 2 trigram frequencies f_{000} and f_{010}, plus the 4 tetragram frequencies f_{0000}, f_{0010}, f_{0100}, and f_{0110}, etc., up to and including the 2^{N-2} N-gram frequencies $f_{0X_1...X_{N-2}0}$; the binary word $X_1...X_{N-2}$ symbolizes the 2^{N-2} possible (N-2)-grams, the X's being logic '1's or '0's.

Proof of the statement is given by induction. First, in Subsection 3.2.3, it is demonstrated that the statement holds for digram frequencies. Later in Subsection 3.2.4 it is demonstrated that if the statement is true for (N-1)-gram frequencies, it is also true for N-gram frequencies.

3.2.2 An Important Relationship. There is one argument that will be used again and again in the following: whenever a M binit binary word $X_1...X_M$ appears in a train of binary digits, it must be preceded by a logic '1' or a logic '0' (when X_1 is not the first digit in the train) and be followed by a logic '1' or a logic '0' (when X_M is not the last digit in the train). Disregarding the end effects the relationships expressed by Equations 3.4 and 3.5 are seen to be true.

$$f_{X_1 \ldots X_M} = f_{0X_1 \ldots X_M} + f_{1X_1 \ldots X_M} \qquad\qquad ; (3.4)$$

$$f_{X_1 \ldots X_M} = f_{X_1 \ldots X_M 0} + f_{X_1 \ldots X_M 1} \qquad\qquad ; (3.5)$$

Unless the opposite is indicated it will be assumed in the remaining part of this report that Equations 3.4 and 3.5 are valid. A consequence of the two equations is that if $X_1 \ldots X_M$ is a string of M logic '1's then $f_{0X_1 \ldots X_M}$ = $f_{X_1 \ldots X_M 0}$ as may be verified by subtraction of Equation 3.4 from Equation 3.5. If $X_1 \ldots X_M$ is a string of M logic '0's it is seen that $f_{1X_1 \ldots X_M}$ = $f_{X_1 \ldots X_M 1}$. This statement may also be verified by subtraction of Equation 3.4 from Equation 3.5. The simplest example of the rules is obtained for M = 1; in this case $f_{10} = f_{01}$.

It should be recalled that the sum of the 2^N N-gram frequencies is unity as mentioned in Section 2.2, Step 4.

3.2.3 Four Digram Frequencies Described by Two Pieces of Information. The two pieces of information are the symbol frequency f_0 and the digram frequency f_{00}. The two frequencies will always satisfy the inequality: $1 \geq f_0 \geq f_{00} \geq 0$. From Equation 3.4 or Equation 3.5 with $X_1 = 0$ and M=1 it is seen that:

$$f_0 = f_{00} + f_{10} \qquad or \qquad f_0 = f_{00} + f_{01}$$

Either expression determines $f_{10} = f_{01}$. The remaining digram frequency, f_{11}, is determined as $f_{11} = 1 - f_{00} - f_{10} - f_{01}$. It has thus been demonstrated that the statement from Subsection 3.2.1 is true for digram frequencies.

3.2.4 2^N N-gram Frequencies Described by 2^{N-1} Pieces of Information.

The 2^{N-1} pieces of information are selected as (1) the frequencies of the 2^{N-2} N-grams that are obtained by taking the 2^{N-2} possible (N-2)-grams and adding a '0' in fromt and a '0' behind the (N-2)-gram, plus (2) the additional 2^{N-2} pieces of information, f_0, f_{00}, etc., which (according to the statement to be proved) permit the computation of the 2^{N-1} frequencies of all possible (N-1)-gram frequencies. It is assumed that the 2^{N-1} (N-1)-gram frequencies have been computed. Some of the (N-1)-gram frequencies will be used in Equations 3.6, 3.7, and 3.8 below.

The 2^N N-gram frequencies (75% of which are as yet undetermined) are divided into 2^{N-2} Blocks of 4 N-gram frequencies each. The 4 N-grams within a Block differ only in their first and/or last digit; they have the general forms: $0X_1 \ldots X_{N-2}0$, $0X_1 \ldots X_{N-2}1$, $1X_1 \ldots X_{N-2}0$ and $1X_1 \ldots X_{N-2}1$ where $X_1 \ldots X_{N-2}$ is one of the 2^{N-2} possible (N-2)-grams. What remains to be shown is that the 3 unknown N-gram frequencies in each Block can be computed from the information available. The three frequencies are computed by Equations 3.6, 3.7, and 3.8 which are similar to Equations 3.4 and 3.5. The frequencies of the (N-1)-grams $0X_1 \ldots X_{N-2}$, $X_1 \ldots X_{N-2}0$ and $X_1 \ldots X_{N-2}1$ have already been computed as mentioned earlier, and the N-gram frequency $f_{0X_1 \ldots X_{N-2}0}$ is one of the selected pieces of information.

$$f_{0X_1 \ldots X_{N-2}1} = f_{0X_1 \ldots X_{N-2}} - f_{0X_1 \ldots X_{N-2}0} \qquad ; (3.6)$$

$$f_{1X_1 \ldots X_{N-2}0} = f_{X_1 \ldots X_{N-2}0} - f_{0X_1 \ldots X_{N-2}0} \qquad ; (3.7)$$

$$f_{1X_1 \ldots X_{N-2}1} = f_{X_1 \ldots X_{N-2}1} - f_{0X_1 \ldots X_{N-2}1} \qquad ; (3.8)$$

This completes the proof by induction of the statement made in Subsection 3.2.1.

3.3 Other Sets of 2^{N-1} Pieces of Information.

The following question may be asked: are there other sets of 2^{N-1} pieces of information that permit the computation of the 2^N N-gram frequencies for an "adequately long" binary sequence? It is obvious that each piece of information should throw new light upon the values of the N-gram frequencies; e.g., 64 hexagram frequencies cannot be computed from 32 pentagram frequencies because the pentagram frequencies constitute, not 32 but only 16 pieces of information.

A set of 2^{N-1} pieces of information that also determine all N-gram frequencies may be obtained in the following manner. Whenever a binary sequence is illustrated by the corresponding path through a flow diagram like Figure 2.2, it will be noticed that from each (N-1)-gram, $'X_1 ..X_{N-1}'$, there is a choice of going to the N-gram $'X_1 \ldots X_{N-1}1'$, or to the N-gram $'X_1 \ldots X_{N-1}0'$ (meaning that there is a choice of adding a '1' or a '0' to the (N-1)-gram). The path has a one-to-one correspondence with the sequence and it can consequently be described in a statistical sense by 2^{N-1} probabilities, one for each branching point. Let the probability of adding a '0' to the (N-1)-gram, $'X_1 \ldots X_{N-1}'$ be $p_{X_1 \ldots X_{N-1}}$.

$$p_{X_1 \ldots X_{N-1}} = f_{X_1 \ldots X_{N-1}0} / f_{X_1 \ldots X_{N-1}} \qquad ; (3.9)$$

The following expression is obtained from Equations 3.5 and 3.9:

$$p_{X_1 \ldots X_{N-1}} = f_{X_1 \ldots X_{N-1}0} / (f_{X_1 \ldots X_{N-1}0} + f_{X_1 \ldots X_{N-1}1}) \qquad ; (3.10)$$

The above expression shows that the 2^{N-1} probabilities can be expressed by the 2^N N-gram frequencies. If a branching point is unused, the corresponding probability is undetermined as indicated by Equation 3.9.

Assume for the moment that <u>all frequencies have values larger than zero.</u> The problem of concern in this section is: can the 2^N N-gram frequencies be computed from the 2^{N-1} probabilities $p_{X_1 \ldots X_{N-1}}$? An affirmative answer to the problem will now be presented in the form of a four step computational procedure.

(1) Write the $(2^{N-1}-1)$ equations that are obtained by letting $X_1 \ldots X_{N-1}$ in Equation 3.11 take the values of all possible (N-1)-grams except the (N-1)-gram, $0 \ldots 0$, consisting of (N-1) '0'-binits. Equation 3.11 can be obtained from Equations 3.4 and 3.5 when M is redefined as (N-1).

$$f_{0X_1 \ldots X_{N-1}} + f_{1X_1 \ldots X_{N-1}} - f_{X_1 \ldots X_{N-1}0} - f_{X_1 \ldots X_{N-1}} = 0 \qquad ; (3.11)$$

(2) Write the 2^{N-1} equations that are obtained by letting $X_1 \ldots X_{N-1}$ in Equation 3.12 take the values of all possible (N-1)-grams.

$$p_{X_1 \ldots X_{N-1}} \cdot f_{X_1 \ldots X_{N-1}1} - (1-p_{X_1 \ldots X_{N-1}}) \cdot f_{X_1 \ldots X_{N-1}0} = 0 \qquad ; (3.12)$$

(3) Add the equation to the system which states that the sum of all 2^N N-gram frequencies is unity.

(4) Solve the 2^N linear equations with 2^N unknowns.

The matrix equation for N=3 is presented as Equation 3.13. The results
of a numerical example are listed in Table 3.1 and the corresponding flow-
diagram is illustrated in Figure 3.1.

The question posed in the first sentence of this section may be
answered as follows: The 2^N N-gram frequencies can be computed from sets
of 2^{N-1} pieces of information that permit the computation of the 2^{N-1}
values of $p_{X_1 \ldots X_{N-1}}$.

Usually each of the 2^{N-1} probabilities has its value located in the
range $(0+\epsilon)$ to $(1-\epsilon)$ where ϵ is defined as an arbitrary small but finite
number. When all sequences are of adequate length, each path in a flow dia-
gram like Figure 2.2 will be used with a finite probability and the first
(N-1) binits from the sequence will recur with a finite probability in the
sequence. The N-gram frequencies are independent of the first (N-1) binits
due to the assumption of adequate length. If some of the frequencies are
zero it may happen that a diagram like Figure 2.2 will be partitioned into
υ regions each of which have the following property: if a path is begun in
the region it will be continued within the region without any excursions
to other regions. In that particular case υ sets of N-gram frequencies will
be valid. E.g., if the four tetragram frequencies f_{1100}, f_{1010}, f_{0101}, and
f_{0011} all are zero, it is seen from Figure 2.2 that the flow diagram is
partitioned into an upper and a lower half. If a path begins in the lower
half (upper half), it will never enter into the upper (lower) half, meaning
that all pentagram frequencies in the upper (lower) half become zero. In
the example υ is equal to two, and two sets of N-gram frequencies are valid.
Which set of frequencies should be used, depends upon the first four binits
in the sequence. The first four binits determine the starting point for
the path and thereby the set of observed frequencies.

$$
\begin{bmatrix} 0 \\ 0 \\ 0 \\ 0 \\ 0 \\ 0 \\ 0 \\ 1 \end{bmatrix}
=
\begin{bmatrix} f_{000} \\ f_{001} \\ f_{010} \\ f_{011} \\ f_{100} \\ f_{101} \\ f_{110} \\ f_{111} \end{bmatrix}
\begin{bmatrix}
0 & 0 & 0 & 0 & 0 & 0 & p_{11} & 1 \\
1 & 0 & -1 & 0 & 0 & 0 & p_{11}{}^{-1} & 1 \\
-1 & 1 & 0 & 0 & 0 & p_{10} & 0 & 1 \\
-1 & 0 & 0 & 0 & 0 & p_{10}{}^{-1} & 0 & 1 \\
0 & -1 & 1 & 0 & p_{01} & 0 & 0 & 1 \\
1 & -1 & 0 & 0 & p_{01}{}^{-1} & 0 & 0 & 1 \\
0 & 1 & 0 & p_{00} & 0 & 0 & 0 & 1 \\
0 & 0 & 0 & p_{00}{}^{-1} & 0 & 0 & 0 & 1
\end{bmatrix}
$$

Equation 3.13

The probability of a '0' following a '11' is $p_{11} = \frac{3}{5}$

The probability of a '0' following a '10' is $p_{10} = \frac{5}{9}$

The probability of a '0' following a '01' is $p_{01} = \frac{7}{13}$

The probability of a '0' following a '00' is $p_{00} = \frac{9}{17}$

$f_{110} = .1169$ $f_{111} = .0779$

$f_{100} = .1407$ $f_{101} = .1125$

$f_{010} = .1363$ $f_{011} = .1168$

$f_{000} = .1582$ $f_{001} = .1407$

The probabilities of the Third Order Machine from Figure 3.1 adding a zero to a digram are listed on the top of the page. The eight trigram frequencies were computed with the help of Equation 3.13.

Table 3.1

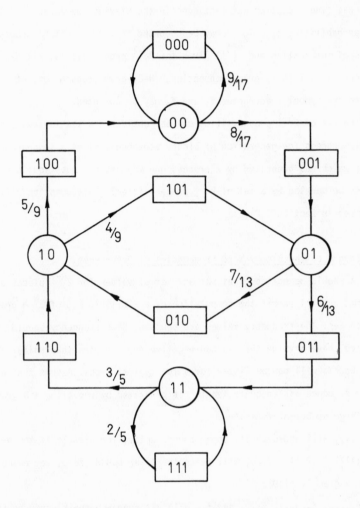

A flowdiagram for a third order machine. The probabilities correspond
to those listed in Table 3.1.

Figure 3.1

The main results obtained in this section are that for most binary sequences (the exception was mentioned in the previous paragraph) (i) the 2^{N-1} probabilities $p_{x_1 \ldots x_{N-1}}$ may be computed from 2^{N-1} suitable chosen pieces of information and (ii) given the 2^{N-1} probabilities, all N-gram frequencies, all (N-1)-gram frequencies, (N-2)-gram frequencies, etc., down to the symbol frequencies f_1 and f_0 may be computed.

The set of 2^{N-1} probabilities may be considered a stationary, stochastic process for generation of binary sequences. Given a sequence of binits which was generated by a process one may ask the question: can the process be modeled by a set of 2^{N-1} probabilities? This question will be discussed in Section 5.2.

3.4 Bounds on the Binary Word Frequencies of Occurrence.

It should be noticed that not any set of values for 2^{N-1} pieces of information will permit the computation of a realistic set of 2^N N-gram frequencies. The frequency values are bounded. Each frequency should, for instance, have a value that is non-negative and not more than unity. The upper bounds will now be listed for a few typical cases. Assume that a binary sequence of "adequate length" is generated by repeating a N-gram a very large number of times:

(1) f_{1111} will approach its upper bound, unity, for example if the N-gram is '1111111' or '1'; f_{1111} will reach the lower bound, zero, for example if the N-gram is '110';

(2) f_{01010}, f_{010101}, f_{101}, and f_{10} will all approach their upper bound, which is $\frac{1}{2}$, if the N-gram is '01';

(3) f_{00100} and f_{00001} will both approach 1/5 if the N-gram is '10000'. 1/5 is the upper bound for f_{00001}. If the N-gram is '100, f_{00100} will ap-

proach its upper bound which is 1/3 and f_{00001} becomes zero;

(4) f_{1-D-0} and f_{0-D-1} are both equal to $f_1-f_{1-D-1} = f_0-f_{0-D-0}$. $\frac{1}{2}$ is consequently an upper bound for f_{1-D-0}. The bound is reached when the N-gram is '01' and D is an odd integer.

It should be noticed that there also exists bounds in form of inequalities. Whenever a binary word Ψ_1 is contained in the word Ψ_2, Ψ_1 will appear at least as many times as Ψ_2 in a binary sequence of "adequate length", meaning that $f_{\Psi_1} \geq f_{\Psi_2}$.

Let Q(T) equal the probability that the signal v(t) generated by a particular random process does not cross the zero axis in a given interval of length T; it is then possible to establish upper bounds for Q(T) (Strakhov and Kurz 1968). Let v(t) be sampled at a constant rate and let positive samples be coded as '1' and non-positive samples be coded as '0'; it is then seen that the upper bounds on Q(T) may be used to establish upper bounds on N-gram frequencies where the N-grams consist of a string of '1's or a string of '0's.

Sometimes, and contrary to the assumption from Subsection 3.2.2, the binary sequence may not be of "adequate length". The sequence could be only five binits long, say, '10011'. This sequence contains one pentagram; f_{10011} is consequently unity, and the 31 other pentagrams have frequencies of occurrence that are zero.

3.5 Redundancy in Delayed N-Gram Frequencies.

It is possible to construct 2^N different binary words that all have a separation of A_1 sampling intervals between digit no. 1 and digit no. 2, A_2 intervals between the next two digits, etc., and A_{N-1} intervals between the last two digits. Such binary words are called delayed N-grams; they were first mentioned in Step no. 8, Section 2.2. Delayed N-grams are the most general kind of binary words. Delayed digrams and N-grams are special cases of delayed N-grams. More than 2^{N-1} pieces of information are usually needed to compute the 2^N frequencies of occurrence of the delayed N-grams. An exception where 2^{N-1} pieces of information determine all 2^N frequencies is encountered, when all (N-1) delays A_1, A_2, ..., and A_{N-1} are of equal duration; in this case the argument from Section 3.2 may be repeated to show that only 2^{N-1} pieces of information are present in the frequencies. In general, the number of pieces of information present in the 2^N frequencies depends upon the relationships between the delays, A_1, A_2, ..., A_{N-1}. Two relationships which are of interest with regard to delayed trigrams will now be presented in Sections 3.6 and 3.7.

3.6 Eight Delayed Trigram Frequencies Contain Five Pieces of Information.

It will be assumed in this section that the two delays, D and E sampling intervals, have different durations, $D \neq E$. The question to be examined is: how many pieces of information are contained in the eight delayed trigram frequencies? The first thing to realize is that the frequency of occurrence of a symbol '0', f_0, is the same no matter whether the first, second or third binit in the trigram is used for the computation of f_0. The following three expressions for f_0 may be obtained by summing over the 4 possible combinations of symbols for the two other binits.

$$f_0 = f_{0-D-1-E-1} + f_{0-D-1-E-0} + f_{0-D-0-E-1} + f_{0-D-0-E-0} \qquad ; (3.14)$$

$$f_0 = f_{1-D-0-E-1} + f_{1-D-0-E-0} + f_{0-D-0-E-1} + f_{0-D-0-E-0} \qquad ; (3.15)$$

$$f_0 = f_{1-D-1-E-0} + f_{1-D-0-E-0} + f_{0-D-1-E-0} + f_{0-D-0-E-0} \qquad\qquad ; (3.16)$$

If the following five pieces of information are known: $f_{0-D-0-E-0}$, $f_{0-D-0-E-1}$, $f_{0-D-1-E-0}$, $f_{1-D-0-E-0}$, and f_0, the three quantities: $f_{0-D-1-E-1}$, $f_{1-D-0-E-1}$, and $f_{1-D-1-E-0}$ may be computed from Equations 3.14, 3.15, and 3.16. Next $f_{1-D-1-E-1}$ can be determined by using the fact that the sum of all eight frequencies is unity. Under the stated assumptions it has been demonstrated that eight delayed trigram frequencies contain five pieces of information. When $D = E$, the eight trigram frequencies contain only four pieces of information; e.g., the trigram frequencies may be determined from: f_0, $f_{0-D-0}(=f_{0-E-0})$, $f_{0-D-1-E-0}$, and $f_{0-D-0-E-0}$ by the procedure described in Section 3.2. In the next section an assumption is introduced which is so restrictive that the eight trigram frequencies contain only three pieces of information.

3.7 A Special Relationship Between Delayed Digrams and Delayed Trigrams.

Consider a binary word Ψ which for the sake of generality will be assumed to be a delayed N-gram. If all '1's in Ψ are replaced by '0's and all '0's in Ψ are replaced by '1's, a new word is generated which will be called $\overline{\Psi}$. In many cases when the mechanisms are known by which the binary sequences are generated, f_Ψ and $f_{\overline{\Psi}}$, for physical reasons, can be expected to have the same value for each sequence. In this particular situation some simple relationships are valid. E.g., an upper bound for f_Ψ becomes $\frac{1}{2}$. As a less obvious example a relationship will be derived that permits the computation of a delayed trigram frequency from the frequencies of the three delayed digrams which are contained in the trigram. Assume that $f_\Psi = f_{\overline{\Psi}}$ for all trigrams with and without delays. The eight trigrams with delays

D, E, and (D+E) have in this case frequencies of occurrence that are completely described by three pieces of information α, β, and γ as may be seen from the expressions 3.17 through 3.20.

$$f_{1-D-1-E-1} = f_{0-D-0-E-0} = \alpha \qquad\qquad ; (3.17)$$

$$f_{1-D-1-E-0} = f_{0-D-0-E-1} = \beta \qquad\qquad ; (3.18)$$

$$f_{1-D-0-E-1} = f_{0-D-1-E-0} = \gamma \qquad\qquad ; (3.19)$$

$$f_{1-D-0-E-0} = f_{0-D-1-E-1} = \frac{1}{2} -\alpha -\beta -\gamma \qquad\qquad ; (3.20)$$

By addition of the proper terms delayed digram frequencies such as those in the Equations 3.21, 3.22, and 3.23 may be obtained.

$$f_{1-D-0} = (f_{1-D-0-E-0} + f_{1-D-0-E-1}) = \frac{1}{2} -\alpha -\beta \qquad\qquad ; (3.21)$$

$$f_{0-E-1} = (f_{0-D-0-E-1} + f_{1-D-0-E-1}) = \beta + \gamma \qquad\qquad ; (3.22)$$

$$f_{1-(D+E)-1} = (f_{1-D-1-E-1} + f_{1-D-0-E-1}) = \alpha + \gamma \qquad\qquad ; (3.23)$$

After elimination of α, β and γ the trigram frequencies can be expressed by the digram frequencies they contain. E.g., through use of Equations 3.19, 3.21, 3.22, and 3.23, $f_{1-D-0-E-1}$ (which is equal to $f_{0-D-1-E-0}$) can be computed from Equation 3.24. Equation 3.24 will be used later in Section 6.2.

$$f_{1-D-0-E-1} = (f_{1-D-0} + f_{0-E-1} + f_{1-(D+E)-1})/2 - \frac{1}{4} \qquad ; (3.24)$$

3.8 The Frequencies of Symmetrical and Unsymmetrical Binary Words.

If a given sequence is scanned first from right to left and then later from left to right, two sets of frequencies of occurrence of the interesting binary words will be obtained. Clearly $f_{X_1...X_N}$ in one set is equal to $f_{X_N...X_1}$ in the other set, just as $f_{X_1-D-X_2-E-X_3}$ in one set is equal to $f_{X_3-E-X_2-D-X_1}$ in the other set, etc. The frequency of a symmetrical word, e.g., f_{10001} or $f_{0-D-1-D-0}$, will have the same value in both sets of frequencies. In general the frequencies of unsymmetrical words, e.g., f_{1101} or $f_{0-D-1-E-1}$ will have different values in the two sets of frequencies; (an exception to this rule was mentioned in the last half of Subsection 3.2.2).

It is seen that the frequencies of symmetrical binary words yield information similar to what is obtained from power spectra, auto-correlation functions, and other "amplitude information" that is independent of the direction in which time is flowing, when the waveform record is read. It is also clear that the frequencies of unsymmetrical binary words contain information related to "phase information"; such information is sensitive to the direction in which time is flowing.

4.   S, A MEASURE OF SEPARABILITY

4.1 Four Statistics.

The following question was posed in Subsection 1.5.4: is there a single-number-statistic that shows how good an attribute, Ξ_i, is for separating members of Class A with the probability density function $f_A = f_A(\Xi_i)$ from members of Class B with the density function $f_B = f_B(\Xi_i)$? Seven measures of separability were mentioned, one of which was the S-measure defined by Equation 4.1.

$$S = |a\text{-}b|/(\sigma_A + \sigma_B) \qquad\qquad ; (4.1)$$

a and σ_A are the mean and standard deviation for f_A. b and σ_B are the mean and standard deviation for f_B. It is the main purpose of this chapter to present a discussion of the S-measure. The discussion is concerned with only one attribute so the subscript "i" will be omitted, $\Xi_i = \Xi$.

Before the S-measure can be discussed, 4 statistics must be introduced. They are defined by Equations 4.4 through 4.7. Let the value of the attribute Ξ be measured for the M_{AD} representative members of Class A. The M_{AD} attribute values called $\xi_1, \xi_2, \ldots, \xi_{M_{AD}}$, are independent and they all come from a population with the distribution f_A. The samples have a sample mean, $\hat{\xi}_A$, and a sample variance, v_A^2; the two moments are defined by Equations 4.2 and 4.3.

$$\hat{\xi}_A = \sum_{j=1}^{M_{AD}} \xi_j / M_{AD} \qquad\qquad ; (4.2)$$

$$v_A^2 = \sum_{j=1}^{M_{AD}} (\xi_j - \hat{\xi}_A)^2 / (M_{AD} - 1) \qquad\qquad ; (4.3)$$

$\hat{\xi}_A$ and v_A^2 are stochastic variables, they have the mean values and variances expressed by Equations 4.4 through 4.8 (Wilks 1962, Section 8.2). $\mu_{4,A}$ defined by Equation 4.8 is the fourth central moment for f_A.

$$\text{Mean}\{\hat{\xi}_A\} \quad = \quad a \qquad\qquad ; (4.4)$$

$$\text{Variance}\{\hat{\xi}_A\} \quad = \quad E\{(\hat{\xi}_A - a)^2\} \quad = \quad \sigma_A^2 / M_{AD} \qquad\qquad ; (4.5)$$

$$\text{Mean}\{v_A^2\} \quad = \quad \sigma_A^2 \qquad\qquad ; (4.6)$$

$$\text{Variance}\{v_A^2\} \quad = \quad (\mu_{4,A} - (M_{AD}-3)\sigma_A^4 / (M_{AD}-1)) / M_{AD} \qquad\qquad ; (4.7)$$

$$\mu_{4,A} \quad = \quad E\{(\Xi-a)^4\} \quad = \quad \int_{-\infty}^{\infty} (\Xi-a)^4 f_A(\Xi) d\Xi \qquad\qquad ; (4.8)$$

If the value of the attribute Ξ is measured for the M_{BD} representative members of Class B similar expressions may be derived for the sample mean, $\hat{\xi}_B$, and sample variance, v_B^2.

4.2 Some Features of the S-Measure.

(1) In practice the designer does not know the values of a, b, σ_A, and σ_B. Therefore, he uses the estimates from Equations 4.4 and 4.6 to obtain the estimate. $\hat{S}$ of S. The statistic $\hat{S}$ is a random variable defined by Equation 4.9.

$$\hat{S} = |\hat{\xi}_A - \hat{\xi}_B| / (v_A + v_B) \qquad\qquad ; (4.9)$$

The designer may estimate the accuracy of the estimate of S with the help of Equations 4.5 and 4.7. The two equations show that as M_{AD} and M_{BD} both approach infinity, $(S-\hat{S})$ goes to zero. In this book it is stated a number of times that the S-value for an attribute is computed from the two sample distributions; strictly speaking, what is done instead is: the estimate of S, $\hat{S}$, is computed with the help of Equation 4.9, and then $\underline{\hat{S} \ is}$ $\underline{used \ instead \ of \ S.}$ Usually, the values of M_{AD} and M_{BD} are so large that the difference $(S-\hat{S})$ is negligible compared to the value of S.

(2) The measure S depends on only the first two moments of f_A and f_B (f_A and f_B being approximated by the two normalized sample distributions). The sixth measure, the Fisher measure, in Subsection 1.5.4 also had this advantage. Very little computer memory per attribute is needed to obtain the four moments $\hat{\xi}_A$, $\hat{\xi}_B$, v_A^2, v_B^2, and to compute $\hat{S}$. When in Block no. 11, Figure 2.1, the many binary word frequencies are determined for each of the M_{AD} plus M_{BD} patterns, it consequently costs little extra memory to compute all the $\hat{S}$ values at the same time. The other five measures of separability require far more computer time and computer memory for their computation.

(3) For $\hat{\xi}_A = \hat{\xi}_B$, $\hat{S}$ becomes zero regardless of how different v_A and v_B may be. Due to this feature, attributes will be discarded (as described in Section 2.3) that well may be of little use when separation is attempted with a hyperplane but which could be of use if separation is attempted with a less simple surface.

(4) Equation 4.1 shows that S, contrary to the Fisher measure, has a linear dependence on $|a-b|$. This important property makes it possible to find relationships among S values for several frequencies of occurrence

of binary words when the frequencies are linearly related. This property
will be used in Sections 5.2 and 5.4.

(5) If Ξ is an effective attribute the two sample distributions should
have few or no regions with high densities in common. The extent to which
this property is present is reflected by any of the seven measures of separability listed in Subsection 1.5.4. To make Ξ a good attribute, it is
furthermore desirable, that the two distributions be essentially unimodal
rather than essentially disjointed as pointed out in Subsection 1.7.2. An
inspection of Figures 1.2 and 1.3 shows that only the Fisher- and the S-
measure from Subsection 1.5.4 reflect the degree to which the distributions
are unimodal, rather than disjointed.

Due to the features listed in Paragraphs (2), (4), and (5), especially (4), it was decided to use the values of the S-measure rather than one
of the other measures for the ordering of attributes in an array as described in Section 2.3.

4.3 A Conjecture, Later Proven by Chernoff

In this subsection it is conjectured that: ordering the attributes
according to decreasing S-values is equivalent to ordering the attributes
according to increasing values of the supremum of the classification error,
C_{sup}. C_{sup} will be defined by Equation 4.16; C_{sup} is the largest possible
classification error given a set of values for $|a-b|$, σ_A and σ_B. Ranking
attributes according to increasing values of C_{sup} is intuitively appealing,
an appeal which under the conjecture is carried over to the ranking according to decreasing S-values. The argument in favor of the conjecture consists of the following four steps; (i) first some constants are specified
by Equations 4.12, 4.13, and 4.14, and (ii) C_{sup} is defined, then (iii)

the densities f_A and f_B in Figure 4.1 are introduced and it is conjectured that C_{sup} is achieved with precisely this configuration; finally (iv) S and C_{sup} are computed for the densities and the relationship

$$C_{sup} = \tfrac{1}{2}/(S^2+1) \qquad\qquad ; (4.10)$$

is obtained; the equation shows that C_{sup} values will increase monotonically with decreasing S-values. For the sake of brevity let $|a-b|$ be called Δ.

$$\Delta = |a-b| \qquad\qquad ; (4.11)$$

(i) The concept of C_{sup} applies when the <u>likelihood decision procedure</u> (Subsection 1.6.4) is used. The following three relationships are consequently valid.

$$K_{AA} = K_{BB} = 0 \qquad\qquad ; (4.12)$$

$$K_{AB} = K_{BA} = 1 \qquad\qquad ; (4.13)$$

$$P_{pr}(A) = P_{pr}(B) = 1/2 \qquad\qquad ; (4.14)$$

One may now ask the following question: given a particular set of values for Δ, σ_A and σ_B, what forms of f_A and f_B would result in the largest average classification cost, C_{mm}?

(ii) It is at this point useful to define the term "Supremum of the Classification Error". When Equations 4.12, 4.13 and 4.14 hold true, the average classification cost (for any specified threshold settings T_1, T_2, etc.) becomes the same as the classification error, C_e. Consider all the pairs of f_A and f_B densities which are possible with a specified set of constraints (in this case the values of $(\Delta, \sigma_A, \sigma_B)$). With any specified (f_A, f_B)-pair is associated many C_e-values depending on where the designer sets his thresholds T_1, T_2, etc. on the Ξ-axis. The smallest possible C_e-value for the specified (f_A, f_B)-pair is called $C_{e,min}$.

$$C_{e,min} = Min\{C_e(\Delta, \sigma_A, \sigma_B)\} \qquad ; (4.15)$$

As (f_A, f_B) scans all the density pairs which satisfy the constraints (which in our case means that they have the specified values for $(\Delta, \sigma_A, \sigma_B)$), a largest (or limiting) value of $C_{e,min}$ will be found. This value is called the supremum of the classification error, C_{sup}.

$$C_{sup} = \underset{f_A, f_B}{Max} \{ Min\{C_e(\Delta, \sigma_A, \sigma_B)\}\} \qquad ; (4.16)$$

Recalling the question at the end of Paragraph (i) it is seen that:

$$C_{mm} = C_{sup} \qquad ; (4.17)$$

the question about the forms of f_A and f_B, however, remains to be answered.

(iii) It is conjectured that the $f_A(\Xi)$ and $f_B(\Xi)$ functions in Figure 4.1 do result in C_{mm}. The value of C_{mm} is given by Equation 4.18.

$$C_{mm} = \tfrac{1}{2}(\sigma_A + \sigma_B)^2/(\Delta^2+(\sigma_A + \sigma_B)^2) \qquad ; (4.18)$$

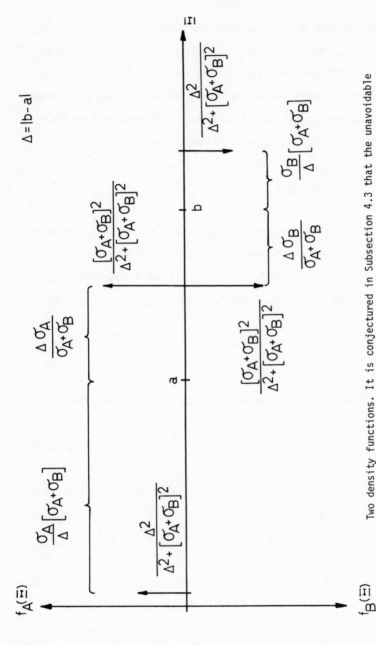

Two density functions. It is conjectured in Subsection 4.3 that the unavoidable classification error (for specified values of Δ, σ_A and σ_B and an unlimited number of thresholds) has been maximized by $f_A(\Xi)$ and $f_B(\Xi)$ illustrated above.

Fig. 4.1

$f_A(\Xi)$ consists of two discrete probabilities $f_A(\Xi_a)$ and $f_A(\Xi_c)$ located at $\Xi=\Xi_a$ and $\Xi=\Xi_c$.

$$\Xi_a = a - \sigma_A (\sigma_A + \sigma_B)/\Delta \qquad\qquad ; (4.19)$$

$$\Xi_c = a + \Delta \sigma_A/(\sigma_A + \sigma_B) \qquad\qquad ; (4.20)$$

$$f(\Xi_a) = \Delta^2/(\Delta^2 + (\sigma_A + \sigma_B)^2) \qquad\qquad ; (4.21)$$

$$f(\Xi_c) = (\sigma_A + \sigma_B)^2/(\Delta^2 + (\sigma_A + \sigma_B)^2) \qquad\qquad ; (4.22)$$

Similarly $f_B(\Xi)$ consists of two discrete probabilities $f_B(\Xi_c)$ and $f_B(\Xi_b)$.

$$\Xi_b = b + \sigma_B (\sigma_A + \sigma_B)/\Delta \qquad\qquad ; (4.23)$$

$$f_B(\Xi_c) = f_A(\Xi_c) \qquad\qquad ; (4.24)$$

$$f_B(\Xi_b) = f_A(\Xi_a) \qquad\qquad ; (4.25)$$

Only one threshold, T_1, is required. T_1 may be located anywhere in range $\Xi_a < T_1 < \Xi_b$. If T_1 falls in the range $\Xi_a < T_1 < \Xi_c$ or $\Xi_c < T_1 < \Xi_b$ it is readily seen that the average cost of classifications has the value from Equation 4.18. If the designer locates T_1 at Ξ_c he must decide how unlabeled patterns with $\Xi=\Xi_c$ should be assigned to Class A and Class B. No matter how the class-assignment is arranged the average cost of misclassifications continues to have the value from Equation 4.18.

(iv) By eliminating $\Delta/(\sigma_A + \sigma_B)$ and C_{mm} between Equations 4.1, 4.17, and 4.18, Equation 4.10 is obtained; it is repeated below.

$$C_{sup} = \tfrac{1}{2}/(S^2 + 1) \qquad\qquad ; (4.10)$$

In summary: ranking of attributes according to increasing C_{sup}-values has intuitive appeal; the ranking of attributes according to decreasing S-values should consequently be equally appealing. The conjecture was first mentioned in 1968 in the first edition of this book; it was later proven by Chernoff (Chernoff 1970).

5.   MODELING OF PATTERN GENERATING STOCHASTIC PROCESSES

5.1 The Importance of a Model.

In Section 2.2, Steps no. 4 through 7, it was described how a number of N-gram frequencies and delayed digram frequencies are examined to determine their value as potential pattern attributes. This is the general procedure that will be used when little or nothing is known about the processes that generated the library of representative patterns.

In many cases the assumption can be made that each of the M_{AD} plus M_{BD} patterns has been generated by a stochastic process, $Z=Z(\phi_1,\phi_2,...)$, with the process parameters ϕ_1, ϕ_2, etc. Depending on the type of process, the number of parameters may be finite, as in the case that will be discussed in Section 5.2, or infinite, as in the case that will be discussed in Section 5.3. When some kind of process Z may be assumed, the search for effective attributes usually can be made substantially more efficient because it is known in advance that effective attributes can be found only among certain kinds of binary word frequencies. If pattern no. 1 was generated by Z, this implies that the pattern is described by its particular set of process parameter values ϕ_{11}, ϕ_{12}, etc. In the same manner each of the other patterns, say pattern no. r, may be described by its particular set of process parameter values ϕ_{r1}, ϕ_{r2}, etc. The categorization problem now has become one of separating the sets of process parameter values that describe the Class A patterns from the sets of process parameter values that describe the Class B patterns. Notice that the parameter values contain information not only about the features that separate the Class A members from the Class B members but also about the features that they have in common. The designer is only concerned with the first kind of information which is found in the "parameters of interest".

Suppose that the designer has been able to justify the assumption that all patterns were generated by processes of type Z. The designer may have used theoretical arguments, measurements on the patterns or both for the justification. After possible preliminary processing as discussed in Subsection 1.5.1, the next step is to sample and code the patterns in such a manner that the values of the parameters of interest will be extractable (to a high degree at least) as frequencies of occurrence of certain binary words. The problem of finding a suitable algorithm was mentioned in Step no. 2, Section 2.2. There is no set procedure for finding an algorithm but the methods used in Sections 5.2 and 5.3 will work in a large number of cases. When the designer succeeds in determining the kind of binary word frequencies that are related to the parameters of interest, he has gained two important advantages.

(1) The set of interesting process parameters will practically always have been expressed by the minimum number of binary word frequencies. Only such frequencies will now have to be computed. E.g., in Subsection 5.2.2 only N-gram frequencies are of interest and in Subsection 5.3.3 only delayed digram frequencies are of interest.

(2) The binary word frequencies will often have acquired a physical meaning. This makes the search for promising new attributes easier to perform; this search will be described in Chapter 6. An example of a simple relationship between binary word frequencies and process parameters will

be presented in Equation 5.13.

Two stochastic processes will be described in Sections 5.2 and 5.3 which are both important candidates for models. The first process generates a stationary random binary Markoff sequence using a transition matrix (Papoulis 1965, pp. 532-535). The second process is the stationary Gaussian process (Papoulis 1965, Sec. 14-2). In Section 5.4 some processes related to the Gaussian process will be discussed. Sometimes the process parameters of interest are related to the shape of the power spectrum. In such situations the designer may find the ρ_0- and ρ_m- concepts of interest; these two concepts are discussed in Section 5.5.

5.2 The Transition Matrix Model.

5.2.1 A Machine for Random Generation of Binits.
To use the FOBW-method it is necessary that the pattern records are sampled and coded according to a suitable algorithm. After coding, each record has been converted into a binary sequence. An example of an algorithm and a possible application will now be presented. Assume that a pattern record has been obtained by letting a subject guess 1000 times whether heads, H, or tails, T, will come up when an unbiased coin is flipped. It is natural to code the binary pattern record HHHTTH... as 111001 where "head"is coded as '1' and "tail" as '0' (Attneave 1959, page 22). Each of such sequences may then be described in a statistical sense by attributes that for instance could be N-gram frequencies of occurrence (Miller and Frick 1949) or delayed digram frequencies of occurrence (Newman and Gerstman 1952). The attribute values illustrate the subject's response pattern.

The results of similar guessing games may in principle be used for

categorization purposes. E.g., monkeys can make binary decisions, therefore, in each monkey's brain there must, so to say, exist a stochastic
process Z for random generation of binits. Monkeys with certain kinds of
brain injuries (hereafter called brain-injured monkeys) have shorter re-
calls than normal monkeys. The brain-injured monkeys generate sequences
that are different from the sequences generated by normal monkeys when
described statistically by binary word frequencies (Leary et al. 1952).
In terms of the material that will be presented in the remaining part of
Section 5.2, the difference between the two classes of sequences is that
the sequence generating processes in the brain-injured monkeys can be
described approximately by certain first order preferences, whereas a
transition matrix of at least size 16 by 16 is needed to model the sequence
generating processes in the normal monkeys. The processes in the brain-
injured monkeys could of course also be modeled by a matrix of size 16 by
16. The probabilities in the matrices will differ from monkey to monkey.
It is now seen that it becomes possible, in principle at least, to classify
an unlabeled sequence as belonging to Class A, "binary sequences generated
by normal monkeys", or as belonging to Class B, "binary sequences generated
by brain-injured monkeys", by taking the following steps. (1) Select a
set of N-gram frequencies which have a one-to-one correspondence with the
probabilities in the sequence generating transition matrix. How this may
be done was described in Section 3.3. The frequencies will be used as
attributes. (Notice that the assumption about the sequence generating
transition matrix makes it possible to pinpoint a comprehensive set of
frequencies). (2) Measure the attribute values for representative members
of Class A and Class B, and for the unlabeled sequence. (3) Classify the
unlabeled sequence as belonging to the class to whose members it is most

similar in terms of the frequency values.

After this example consider again the case where a binary sequence
has been generated by sampling and coding of a pattern. The question may
now be asked: is there a conceptually simple kind of machine that could
have generated the same sequence? In this subsection a possible machine
will be described that in a stationary random manner will generate a
binary sequence. The machine has the important feature that its parameters,
the probabilities in a transition matrix, can be determined from the N-
gram frequencies of the sequences it generates. To make an Nth-order
machine of this type work, two things are needed. (i) (N-1) binary digits.
They constitute the first (N-1) binits of the binary sequence and are
needed to give the machine a starting point. (ii) The probability of the
machine adding a logic '0', rather than a logic '1', to a train of binits.
The machine is so constructed that this probability depends exclusively
upon the last (N-1) digits in the train of binits. 2^{N-1} probabilities are
therefore needed to describe the machine as was explained in Section 3.3.
In this section the values of the probabilities are <u>assumed</u> to remain
constant in time.

As an example, consider the case N=3. To start the machine two binits
are needed. Assume that in some manner the two binits '01' have been
selected. The machine can now add a '0' or a '1' to '01'. Let the probability that it chooses a '0' be 7/13, and that it chooses a '1' be 6/13.
In the first case the last three binits of the train of binits would constitute the trigram '010', in the second case they would constitute the
trigram '011'. A set of 4 probabilities for a third order machine has
been listed in Table 3.1. The corresponding flow-diagram is shown in
Figure 3.1 and the transition matrix is shown in Figure 5.1.

5.2.2 The N-Gram Frequencies Determine all Other Binary Word Frequencies.

In Section 3.3 it was shown that there is a well-defined relationship between the 2^{N-1} probabilities $p_{X_1 \ldots X_{N-1}}$ that describe the Nth-order machine and the N-gram frequencies. It could therefore be expected that all other binary word frequencies can be computed from the N-gram frequencies. That this is actually the case will now be demonstrated by dividing the remaining binary word frequencies into 3 groups: M-gram frequencies where M>N, M-gram frequencies where M<N, and the delayed M-gram frequencies. For each group it will be demonstrated that the binary word frequencies can be computed from the N-gram frequencies.

(1) M-gram frequencies, M>N. Two things must happen before a certain (N+1)-gram, say $X_1 X_2 \ldots X_N 0$, can appear in a train of binits; $X_1 \ldots X_N$ are N binary digits. First the N-gram $X_1 X_2 \ldots X_N$ must be present, it has a frequency of occurrence that is $f_{X_1 X_2 \ldots X_N}$. Secondly, the machine must decide to add '0' to the train of binits following X_N. The addition of '0' will occur with probability:

$$p_{X_2 X_3 \ldots X_N} = f_{X_2 X_3 \ldots X_N 0} / (f_{X_2 X_3 \ldots X_N 0} + f_{X_2 X_3 \ldots X_N 1}) \qquad ; (5.1)$$

according to the definition from Equation 3.9. The addition of a '1' will occur with probability

$$1 - p_{X_2 X_3 \ldots X_N} = f_{X_2 X_3 \ldots X_N 1} / (f_{X_2 X_3 \ldots X_N 0} + f_{X_2 X_3 \ldots X_N 1}) \qquad ; (5.2)$$

The value of $p_{X_2 X_3 \ldots X_N}$ is independent of whether X_1 was '1' or '0'. The frequency with which $X_1 X_2 \ldots X_N 0$ occurs among the (N+1)-grams in the sequence is consequently determined by Equation 5.3.

Binits number n and (n+1) in the sequence

		11	10	01	00
	11	2/5	3/5	0	0
Binits number (n-1) and n in the sequence	10	0	0	4/9	5/9
	01	6/13	7/13	0	0
	00	0	0	8/17	9/17

This transition matrix shows the probability that the digram consisting of the last two digits, binits number (n-1) and n, in the sequence will generate the digram consisting of binits number n and (n+1); the probabilities are the same as those for the Third Order Machine in Table 3.1 and Figure 3.1. A matrix for an Nth order machine has size 2^{N-1} by 2^{N-1}. The matrix is determined by 2^{N-1} probabilities, $p_{X_1...X_{N-1}}$ as discussed in Section 3.3.

Figure 5.1

$$f_{X_1X_2\ldots X_N0} = f_{X_1X_2\ldots X_N} \cdot \frac{f_{X_2X_3\ldots X_N0}}{f_{X_2X_3\ldots X_N0} + f_{X_2X_3\ldots X_N1}} \qquad ; (5.3)$$

Equation 5.3 shows that the (N+1)-gram frequencies can be computed from the N-gram frequencies.

The frequencies of occurrence of (N+2)-grams may also be computed from the N-gram frequencies by using the described technique twice. For instance, the frequency of occurrence of $X_1X_2\ldots X_N01$ is determined by Equation 5.4 where $f_{X_1X_2\ldots X_N0}$ may be computed with the help of Equation 5.3.

$$f_{X_1X_2\ldots X_N01} = f_{X_1X_2\ldots X_N0} \cdot \frac{f_{X_3\ldots X_N01}}{f_{X_3\ldots X_N01} + f_{X_3\ldots X_N00}} \qquad ; (5.4)$$

The frequencies of occurrence of M-grams, M>N, obviously can be computed from the N-gram frequencies by repeated multiplication with factors like the right hand sides of Equations 5.1 and 5.2.

(2) M-gram frequencies, M<N. The frequencies of occurrence of (N-1)-grams are obtained by adding 2 N-gram frequencies. $f_{X_1X_2\ldots X_{N-1}}$ may be obtained from Equation 5.5 or Equation 5.6. Equations 5.5 and 5.6 are similar to Equations 3.4 and 3.5.

$$f_{X_1X_2\ldots X_{N-1}} = f_{X_1X_2\ldots X_{N-1}0} + f_{X_1X_2\ldots X_{N-1}1} \qquad ; (5.5)$$

$$f_{X_1X_2\ldots X_{N-1}} = f_{0 X_1X_2\ldots X_{N-1}} + f_{1 X_1X_2\ldots X_{N-1}} \qquad ; (5.6)$$

By adding pairs of (N-1)-gram frequencies, (N-2)-gram frequencies are

obtained, etc. The frequencies of occurrence of M-grams, M<N, obviously
can be obtained from the N-gram frequencies by simple addition.

(3) Delayed M-gram frequencies. The frequencies of occurrence of delayed
M-grams can also be computed from the N-gram frequencies. For instance,
the frequency of occurrence of a '1' followed D sampling intervals later
by a '0' and an additional E sampling intervals later by a '1', $f_{1-D-0-E-1}$,
may be computed as follows. List the binary words which are (D+E+1) binits
long, and which have '1' as digit no. 1, '0' as digit no. (D+1), and '1'
as the last digit. There are 2^{D+E-2} such binary words and they are the
only (D+E+1)-grams containing the delayed trigram '1-D-0-E-1'. Compute
the frequency of occurrence for each of the words. The sum of the 2^{D+E-2}
frequencies is $f_{1-D-0-E-1}$.

Based on Section 3.3 and Subsections 5.2.1 and 5.2.2, and under the
stated assumptions it is seen that a binary sequence which has been
generated by a stationary transition matrix of size 2^{N-1} by 2^{N-1} is
completely described in a statistical sense by a suitable set of 2^{N-1}
binary word frequencies of occurrence. The underlined statement constitutes
the main result of Section 5.2.

5.2.3 Testing the Applicability of the Model. The problem that will be
discussed in this subsection may be stated as follows: when a binary
sequence is available that was generated by a stationary stochastic process, how does one decide if the process can be modeled by a stationary
transition matrix, 2^{N-1} by 2^{N-1} of size? The answer is obtained in the
following manner.

(1) First the frequencies of occurrence of symbols, digrams, trigrams,
etc., up to, say, 8-binit words are computed from the binary sequence.

(2) The hypothesis is tested that the process may be described by a transition matrix of 0-order meaning that the symbol frequency f_0 alone controls the generation of the sequence. If the hypothesis is true (as it was for the brain-injured monkeys, Subsection 5.2.1), the following statements with regard to the measured digram frequencies must be true.

$$f_{11} = (1-f_0)^2, \; f_{10} = f_{01} = f_0 \cdot (1-f_0) \text{ and } f_{00} = (f_0)^2$$

If the mathematical statements above are found to be false by inspection of the actual digram frequencies, proceed to Step no. 3 below. If the statements are found to be true, a new set of statements with regard to the measured trigram frequencies are checked.

$$f_{111} = (1-f_0)^3, \; f_{011} = f_{101} = f_{110} = (1-f_0)^2 \cdot f_0,$$

$$f_{001} = f_{010} = f_{100} = (f_0)^2 \cdot (1-f_0) \text{ and } f_{000} = (f_0)^3$$

If the above set of statements are found to be false by inspection of the actual trigram frequencies, proceed to Step no. 3. If the statements are found to be true, test the hypothesis on the tetragram level. If the hypothesis holds on the tetragram level, test it on the pentagram level, etc. The number of levels that should be used in the testing could for instance be determined as the number of sampling intervals that correspond to the apparent de-correlation time of the process. In practice it may not be possible to compute more than a few thousand frequencies of occurrence; consequently, the number of levels where the first order machine hypothesis can be tested may be limited by the available frequencies.

If the hypothesis holds on all available levels it should be accepted as a good working hypothesis. Also it should be studied if there are theoretical reasons why the process apparently can be modeled by a 0-order transition matrix.

(3) The hypothesis is tested that the process may be described by a second order machine meaning that a transition matrix 2 by 2 of size alone controls the generation of the sequence. The assumption is now that the probability of adding a '0' to the train of binits depends only on the last digit in the train. If the last digit is '1', the probability is $p_1 = f_{10}/(f_{10} + f_{11})$; if the last digit is '0', the probability is $p_0 = f_{00}/(f_{00} + f_{01})$. When the hypothesis is true, the following statements with regard to the actually measured trigram frequencies must be true. The mathematical statements are obtained by using Equations 5.1 through 5.6.

$$f_{111} = f_{11} \cdot \frac{f_{11}}{f_{10} + f_{11}} \ , \ f_{001} = f_{100} = f_{10} \cdot \frac{f_{00}}{f_{00} + f_{01}} \ ,$$

$$f_{110} = f_{011} = f_{01} \cdot \frac{f_{11}}{f_{10} + f_{11}} \ , \ f_{000} = f_{00} \cdot \frac{f_{00}}{f_{00} + f_{01}} \ ,$$

$$f_{010} = f_{01} \cdot \frac{f_{10}}{f_{10} + f_{11}} \ \text{and} \ f_{101} = f_{10} \cdot \frac{f_{01}}{f_{00} + f_{01}}$$

If the statements are found to be in agreement with the measured trigram frequencies, the hypothesis is tested on the tetragram level as the next step, etc.

If the hypothesis holds on all available levels, a good working hypothesis has been found. It should then be studied why the simple transition matrix model seems to describe the process so well.

(4) In the described manner, the hypothesis of larger and larger
transition matrices may be tested against measured frequencies. As it
becomes necessary to hypothesize larger and larger values for the order
of the transition matrix, two things will happen. More and more probabilities, 2^{N-1} probabilities, are needed to determine the 2^N non-zero
elements in the matrix. Also, the performance will be better in the
cases where the dependence between binits in the sequence decrease with
the number of sampling intervals that separate the binits. If, for instance, the dependence has become negligible between binits that are
separated by D or more sampling intervals, then the stationary process
can be modeled by a Dth order transition matrix of the type illustrated
in Figure 5.1. A Dth order transition matrix has 2^{D-1} by 2^{D-1} entries.

5.3 The Gaussian Process Model.

5.3.1 The Examination of the Bivariate Distribution. When waveform
records have been obtained that were generated by a stationary, stochastic
process it may be asked what the nature was of the process. Certain processes may be completely described by the bivariate probability density
function of their time sampled records, the most important of such processes being the Gaussian or normal process (Middleton 1960, Chapter 7).
Although only the Gaussian process will be discussed, some of the techniques presented here in Section 5.3 may applay to other processes that
are defined by their bivariate probability density function. It is assumed
that each waveform record is so long that it after sampling and coding
constitutes a binary sequence of "adequate length" as defined in Section

3.1; the question of how long the waveform record should be will be taken up in Subsection 5.3.5. It is possible to test the hypothesis that a waveform record has been generated by a Gaussian process; it could, for instance, be done with a Chi-squared test (Hald 1962, Sec. 23.2).

5.3.2 The Gaussian Bivariate Distribution.

Let a stationary waveform record, generated by a Gaussian process, be impulse sampled at a constant rate at the instants $t=n\cdot\pi/\omega$; n is an integer in the range $0\leq n<\infty$ and π/ω is a constant. Then the pairs of samples (v_1, v_2) that have a separation in time of $\tau=D\pi/\omega$ will have the bivariate distribution $P(v_1,v_2; D\pi/\omega)$ as expressed by Equation 5.8 and illustrated by Figure 5.2 (Middleton 1960, Section 7.2). The auto-correlation function for the waveform before sampling is called $R(\tau)$, the process mean m, the variance σ^2, and the correlation coefficient $\rho(\tau)$. The quantities are related to each other by Equations 5.9 and 5.10.

$$\tau = D\pi/\omega$$

$$\rho = \rho(\tau) \qquad\qquad ; (5.7)$$

$$P(v_1,v_2;\tau) = \frac{\exp\left(-\dfrac{(v_1-m)^2 + (v_2-m)^2 - 2\rho(v_1-m)(v_2-m)}{2\sigma^2(1-\rho^2)}\right)}{2\pi\sigma^2\sqrt{1-\rho^2}} \qquad ; (5.8)$$

$$R(0) = \sigma^2\left(1+(m/\sigma)^2\right) \qquad\qquad ; (5.9)$$

$$R(\tau) = \sigma^2\left(\rho + (m/\sigma)^2\right) \qquad\qquad ; (5.10)$$

Let the waveform samples be coded according to the following coding algorithm called the "sign algorithm": all positive samples are described by a logic '1', all non-positive samples are described by a logic '0'. One important result immediately becomes obvious when this algorithm is used: the probability mass in the first quadrant of Figure 5.2, meaning the probability of a positive sample being followed D sampling intervals later by another positive sample, has the value f_{1-D-1}; the probability mass in the third quadrant likewise has the value f_{0-D-0}.

5.3.3 The Relationship Between m/σ,ρ, and the Delayed Digram Frequencies.

In the last paragraph of the previous subsection the equivalence between delayed digram frequencies and values of probability masses was established In this Subsection it will be shown how the probability masses are related to the familiar parameters m/σ and ρ.

It may be shown that the first quadrant probability mass, f_{1-D-1}, and the third quadrant probability mass, f_{0-D-0}, can be expressed by Equations 5.11 and 5.12. Families of curves illustrating the L-function are available in the literature (Abramowitz and Stegun 1964, Equation 26.3.20).

$$f_{1-D-1} = 2L(- \frac{m}{\sigma} , 0, - \sqrt{(1-\rho)/2} \; \text{sgn} \, (m/\sigma)) \qquad ; (5.11)$$

$$f_{0-D-0} = 2L(\frac{m}{\sigma} , 0, - \sqrt{(1-\rho)/2} \; \text{sgn} \, (m/\sigma)) \qquad ; (5.12)$$

The diagram in Figure 5.3 was obtained by plotting constant values, first of f_{1-D-1} and later of f_{0-D-0} against m/σ and $\sqrt{(1-\rho)/2}$. The diagram can be used to determine m/σ and ρ from f_{1-D-1} and f_{0-D-0}. The procedure is as follows:

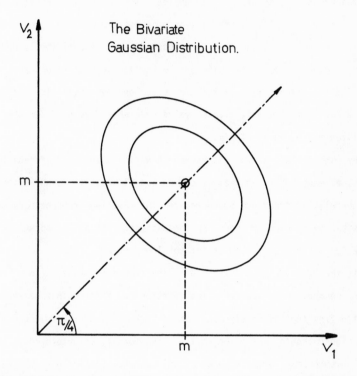

The elliptical contours illustrate points with constant bivariate
probability density as expressed by Equation 5.8. m is the mean value
of both v_1 and v_2. The correlation between v_1 and v_2 is negative on
the figure.

Figure 5.2

(1) measure f_{1-D-1} and f_{0-D-0} and decide which is the larger. If f_{1-D-1} is the larger it implies that the mean m is positive.

(2) locate the two curves that correspond to the value of the larger valued frequency and to the value of the smaller valued frequency.

(3) find the intersection of the two curves and determine its coordinates m/σ and ρ. If $f_{0-D-0} > f_{1-D-1}$ the value $-m/\sigma$ should be used for the normalized mean instead of m/σ.

By repeated use of the diagram and Equation 5.10 for different D-values, as many points as desired can be established on the normalized auto-correlation function; by increasing the sampling frequency ω/π the points can be as closely spaced as the designer wishes. The normalization can be for AC power, $\sigma^2 = 1$, or for total power, $R(0) = 1$.

If the process is band-limited to the frequency range $-\omega$ to $+\omega$ radians/second, the autocorrelation function may in principle be reconstructed from the infinitely many samples $R(D\pi/\omega)$ and $R(-D\pi/\omega)$, $0 \leq D < \infty$. If the designer should want to reconstruct the normalized autocorrelation function some small but finite error will be unavoidable in practical cases; some possible error sources are: the finite record length and the aliasing of frequency components above $\omega/(2\pi)$ (Papoulis 1966). The auto-correlation function and the mean describe the stationary Gaussian process completely; in other words: disregarding a constant for power normalization a Gaussian process can be described by the delayed digram frequencies of an "adequately long", sampled and coded waveform record.

Diagrams like the one in Figure 5.3 may also be constructed for other bivariate distributions which, like the power-normalized Gaussian distribution, depend on only two parameters. If the two parameters are called $p_1(D)$ and $p_2(D)$, the diagram should relate (f_{1-D-1}, f_{0-D-0}) and $(p_1(D), p_2(D))$.

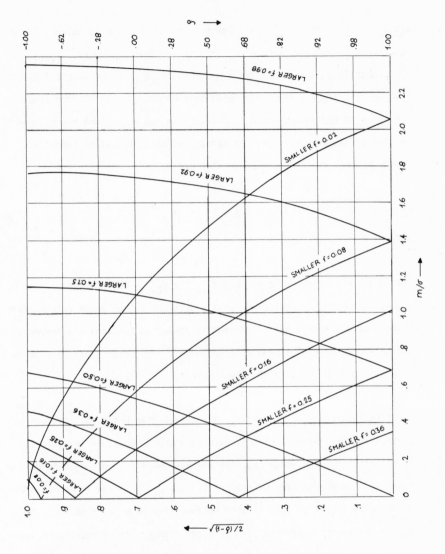

A diagram relating f_{1-D-1} and f_{0-D-0} to m/σ and ρ. The diagram is described in Subsection 5.3.3.

Figure 5.3

5.3.4 The Case with Zero Mean. For m=0 it may be shown by integration of Equation 5.8 that the probability mass in the first quadrant, f_{1-D-1}, and the probability mass in the third quadrant, f_{0-D-0}, both are equal to $\frac{1}{4}$ + (arc $\sin\rho$)/(2π), (Papoulis 1965, Section 14.4). Specializing Equations 5.9 and 5.10 for the case m=0, the following two equivalent expressions in closed form are obtained. The normalized autocorrelation function simply becomes the correlation coefficient ρ.

$$R(D\pi/\omega)/R(0) = \sin(2\pi(f_{1-D-1} - \frac{1}{4}))$$

$$\rho(D\pi/\omega) = -\cos(2\pi f_{1-D-1}) \qquad\qquad ; (5.13)$$

Due to the assumption of zero mean, $f_{1-D-1} = f_{0-D-0}$ has a value between 0 and $\frac{1}{2}$. Equation 5.13 does consequently describe a one-to-one relationship between points on the normalized auto-correlation function and the delayed digram frequencies. The same relationship is presented in graphical form in Figure 5.3 on the straight line where $f_{1-D-1} = f_{0-D-0}$.

5.3.5 Estimation of the Normalized Autocorrelation Function. In this subsection the following problem is examined: when a waveform is generated by a stationary, zero-mean Gaussian process, what record length is needed to make a "good estimate" of $\rho(D\pi/\omega)$ from f_{1-D-1}? The designer is interested in an answer to this problem because it will make it possible for him to relate the unfamiliar binary words frequencies of occurrence to points, $\rho(D\pi/\omega)$, on the familiar autocorrelation function. The relationship between f_{1-D-1} and points on the normalized autocorrelation function, $\rho(D\pi/\omega)$, is given by Equation 5.13. In this subsection the following simplified nomenclature will be used to save space:

$f = f_{1-D-1}$ and $r = \rho(D\pi/\omega)$. Equation 5.13 is rewritten as Equation 5.14.

$$r = -\cos 2\pi f \qquad\qquad ; \ (5.14)$$

A reasonable estimate $\hat{r}$ of r is given by Equation 5.15.

$$\hat{r} = -\cos 2\pi\hat{f} \qquad\qquad ; \ (5.15)$$

$\hat{f}$ is defined as the observed value of f for the record of length T. The expected value of $\hat{f}$ is f.

First we are interested in getting an idea of the variance of $\hat{f}$, var $(\hat{f})$. The record is therefore divided into N segments each of length L, $T = N \cdot L$, and the value of f is computed for each segment. The segment length L should correspond to several times the decorrelation time so that the N observed values of f: $f_1, f_2, \ldots, f_k, \ldots f_N$ may be assumed to be independent. Recalling the definition of a binary word frequency from Section 2.2, Step no. 4, it is seen that the estimate $\hat{f}$ is the mean of $f_1, f_2, \ldots, f_N$.

$$\hat{f} = \frac{1}{N} \sum_{k=1}^{N} f_k \qquad\qquad ; \ (5.16)$$

Each of the independent random variables $f_1, \ldots, f_N$ has f as the expected value. Let $E\{\cdot\}$ indicate the operation of finding the expected value. The variance of $\hat{f} = E\{(f-\hat{f})^2\}$ may be obtained from Equation 5.17 or from Equation 5.18 recalling the assumed independence of $f_1, \ldots, f_N$.

$$\text{var}\{\hat{f}\} = E\{\frac{1}{N}2 \cdot \sum_{m=1}^{N} \sum_{k=1}^{N} (f-f_k)(f-f_m)\} \qquad ; \ (5.17)$$

$$\text{var } \{\hat{f}\} = \frac{1}{N} \cdot \text{var}\{f_k\} \qquad\qquad ; (5.18)$$

The variance of f_k, $\text{var}\{f_k\}$, is defined as

$$\text{var}\{f_k\} = E\{(f_k - f)^2\} = E\{((f_k - \hat{f}) + (\hat{f} - f))^2\}.$$

$$\text{var}\{f_k\} = E\{(f_k - \hat{f})^2\} + 2E\{(f_k - \hat{f})(\hat{f} - f)\} + E\{(\hat{f} - f)^2\} \qquad ; (5.19)$$

The leftmost term on the right hand side of Equation 5.19 is the only term that can be measured, the other two terms contain the unknown quantity f. The second term is zero; this may be seen in the following manner. For any given $\hat{f}$-value the summation on the left hand side of Equation 5.20 has zero as the result due to Equation 5.16. The value of the second term on the right hand side of Equation 5.19 is twice the expected value of a product which is zero; the second term is consequently zero:

$$(\hat{f} - f) \cdot \sum_{k=1}^{N} (f_k - \hat{f})/N = (\hat{f} - f) \cdot 0 \qquad\qquad ; (5.20)$$

The third term on the right hand side of Equation 5.19 is $\text{var}\{\hat{f}\} = \text{var}\{f_k\}/N$ according to Equation 5.18. Equation 5.19 may now be rewritten as Equation 5.21.

$$\text{var}\{f_k\} = E\{(f_k - \hat{f})^2\} + \text{var}\{f_k\}/N \qquad\qquad ; (5.21)$$

Consequently, the variance of $\hat{f}$ is:

$$\text{var}\{\hat{f}\} = \frac{1}{N(N-1)} \sum_{k=1}^{N} (f_k - \hat{f})^2 \qquad\qquad ; (5.22)$$

It remains to relate the variance of $\hat{f}$ to the mean-square error of $\hat{r}$. Let ε be defined as $\varepsilon = \hat{f}-f$. ε is a zero-mean random variable. It is seen from Equations 5.14 and 5.15 that:

$$|\hat{r}-r| = |\cos 2\pi\hat{f} - \cos 2\pi f| =$$

$$|2\pi\varepsilon \cdot \frac{\cos 2\pi(f+\varepsilon) - \cos 2\pi f}{2\pi\varepsilon}| \cong 2\pi |\varepsilon \sin 2\pi f| \leq 2\pi |\varepsilon|.$$

$$E\{(\hat{r}-r)^2\} \leq (2\pi\varepsilon)^2 = 4\pi^2 \cdot \text{var}\{\hat{f}\}.$$

Substituting Equation 5.22 into the above expression a higher bound is obtained for the mean square error or $\hat{r}$. The error is at most:

$$E\{(\hat{r}-r)^2\} = \frac{4\pi^2}{N(N-1)} \sum_{k=1}^{N} (f_k - \hat{f})^2 \qquad ; \quad (5.23)$$

With Equation 5.23 the designer can decide from $f_1 \ldots, f_N$ if the coded record of length T is long enough to make "a good estimate" of $r=\rho(D\pi/\omega)$. The designer wants each coded waveform record to be so long that he can make "good estimates" of $r=\rho(D\pi/\omega)$ for all D-values of interest.

5.3.6 The Delayed Digram Frequencies Determine all Other Binary Word Frequencies.

After a waveform record, $v=v(t)$, has been sampled at the instants $n\pi/\omega$, n=1, 2, 3, etc., it is possible to determine a multitude of multivariate distribution functions. E.g., the distribution of the values of four samples, $v(n\pi/\omega)$, $v((n+D)\pi/\omega)$, $v((n+D+E)\pi/\omega)$, and $v((n+D+E+F)\pi/\omega)$, which follow each other with delays of $D\pi/\omega$, $E\pi/\omega$, and $F\pi/\omega$ could be determined. In the example with four samples, the probability mass would be divided among $2^4 = 16$ orthants. If the samples are coded according to the sign algorithm it becomes obvious that each of the

16 possible frequencies of occurrence of tetragrams with delays D, E, and F, e.g., $f_{1-D-1-E-1-F-1}$, is equal to the probability mass in one of the 16 orthants. By generalizing from the example it is seen that the frequency of occurrence of any delayed N-gram is equal to the probability mass in one of the 2^N orthants for the corresponding multivariate sample distribution in N-dimensional space. The probability mass in an orthant stays constant during a power normalization where all the samples are multiplied by a constant. It may without loss of generality be assumed in the remaining part of this subsection that $\sigma=1$. After this introductory remark, the following problem will be examined: can all binary word frequencies be determined from the delayed digram frequencies?

First, it will be demonstrated that the question can be answered in the affirmative when zero mean may be assumed for the Gaussian process, m=0. In this case delayed trigram frequencies may be determined by expressions like Equation 3.16. Equation 3.16 is incidentally valid, not only for the zero-mean Gaussian case, but for any kind of trivariate distribution where $f_\psi = f_{\bar\psi}$; this was demonstrated in Section 3.7. It is important to determine how the frequency of occurrence of a delayed N-gram can be computed because the delayed N-gram is the most general binary word. In its general form the delayed N-gram includes ordinary N-grams and all other binary words. It will therefore suffice to demonstrate that delayed N-gram frequencies may be computed from the delayed digram frequencies. This is done by taking the following steps. (1) First it is determined which digrams are contained in the delayed N-gram. E.g., the delayed tetragram 1-D-1-E-1-F-1 contains the six delayed digrams: 1-D-1, 1-(D+E)-1, 1-(D+E+F)-1, 1-E-1, 1-(E+F)-1, 1-F-1. (2) The corresponding correlation coefficients, e.g., $\rho(D\pi/\omega)$, etc., are obtained from the digram frequencies through use of Figure 5.3 or Equation 5.13. (3) The approximate value of the probability mass in the orthant of interest is determined from the correlation coefficients (Bacon 1963, Equation 13). The accuracy of the computation will be sufficient for applications with the FOBW method. As pointed out in the beginning of this subsection, the probability mass in the orthant is equal to the desired, delayed N-gram frequency.

In the case with <u>non-zero mean</u>, $m \neq 0$, it will be noticed that the power normalized Gaussian multivariate sample distribution with N variables is completely described by $N(N-1)/2$ correlation coefficients and m/σ (Middleton 1960, Section 7.3). The $N(N-1)/2+1$ quantities are readily determined from $N(N-1)/2+1$ delayed digram frequencies. With reference to the example with the delayed tetragram, 1-D-1-E-1-F-1, it is seen that the seven quantities may be determined from f_{0-D-0} plus the frequencies of occurrence of the six delayed digrams mentioned in the previous paragraph. The procedure is as follows, exemplified by the tetragram case. (1) f_{0-D-0} and f_{1-D-1} determine m/σ and $\rho(D\pi/\omega)$ per Figure 5.3. (2) m/σ, which was just determined, and $f_{1-(D+E)-1}$ determine $\rho((D+E)\pi/\omega)$ per Figure 5.3. (3) The remaining four correlation coefficients are likewise determined from Figure 5.3 by m/σ and the corresponding digram frequencies. After the power normalized multivariate distribution has been obtained, the probability mass in each of the 2^4 orthants may be determined by numerical methods.

The procedures exemplified by the tetragram apply to all delayed N-gram frequencies. The question posed at the end of the first paragraph of this subsection may consequently be answered in the affirmative. The main result of this subsection is that <u>if the set of infinitely many delayed</u>

digram frequencies is known for a stationary Gaussian process all other binary word frequencies in principle can be obtained. In practice it is usually sufficient to compute digrams with delays up to D_{max} where $D_{max} \dot{=} \pi/\omega$ is a few times the decorrelation time for the Gaussian process.

5.4 Processes Related to the Gaussian Process.

The diagram, Figure 5.3, is useful in some other situations that now will be described.

5.4.1 A Special Type of Transmission Path.

Sometimes it may not be possible to sample the undistorted waveform that was generated by a Gaussian process; only after the waveform has been distorted during transmission does it become available for sampling. For a particular type of transmission path it is still possible to recover points on the normalized autocorrelation function as if no distortion had taken place. Figure 5.4 illustrates the path, it consists of a constant time delay, t_0, followed by a memoryless, nonlinear, timevarying device with input V_{in} and output V_{out}.

$$V_{out} = f(V_{in}, t) \qquad\qquad ; (5.24)$$

The device should have the following two properties.

(1) V_{out} increases monotonically with V_{in}

(2) $V_{in} = K_1$ does at all times result in $V_{out} = K_2$; K_1 and K_2 are two constants both of which could be zero.

Let the undistorted waveform be called $g_w(t)$. The output signal from the device is called $h_w(t-t_0)$ and may look quite different from $g_w(t)$. However, if $h_w(t-t_0)$ is sampled at a constant rate and the samples are

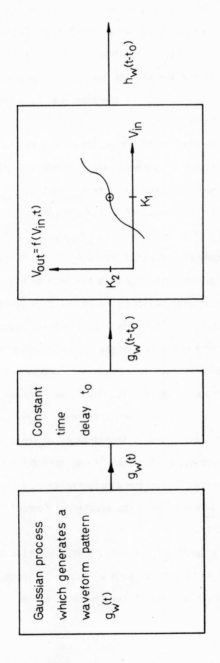

Transmission Path discussed in Subsection 5.4.1

Figure 5.4

coded according to the K_2-algorithm: "all samples larger than K_2 are described by a logic 1, all other samples are described by a logic 0", the
same binary sequence is obtained as if $g_w(t-t_0)$ had been sampled at the
same instants and the samples had been coded according to the K_1-algorithm
"all samples larger than K_1 are described by a logic 1, all other samples
are described by a logic 0".

A consequence of this observation may be stated as follows: assume
that (1) instead of representative waveform patterns $g_{w,1}(t)$, $g_{w,2}(t)$,
etc., only the distorted patterns $h_{w,1}(t-t_0)$, $h_{w,2}(t-t_0)$, etc., are available, and (2) the value of K_2 for the common transmission path is known.
If so, pairs of delayed digrams, (f_{1-D-1}, f_{0-D-0}), derived from a $h_w(t-t_0)$
waveform, sampled and coded according to the K_2-algorithm, can be determined. The digram pairs may with the help of Figure 5.3 be used to determine points on a normalized auto-correlation function; the normalization
is performed by selecting $\sigma^2=1$. This auto-correlation function differs only
by a constant amount, K_1, in the mean value from the normalized auto-correlation function that could have been determined from the $g_w(t-t_0)$ or
$g_w(t)$ waveforms if the sampled waveforms had been coded according to the
sign algorithm. This constant difference is the same for all members of
Class A and Class B and is therefore of no consequence for the design of
a pattern recognizer. A pattern recognizer designed to classify $h_w(t-t_0)$
type patterns will give the same performance as one designed to classify
$g_w(t)$ type patterns (when the functional form of the separation surface
is unrestricted).

In many practical situations the connection between the sensor and
the PR must be brought through a hostile environment. It has been shown
in this subsection that if the designer intends to use the sign algorithm,

he only has to establish a transmission path through the hostile environment which is a close approximation to the one illustrated in Figure 5.4.
In most realistic cases K_1 and K_2 will both be zero.

5.4.2 Additive Gaussian Noise. Let stationary Gaussian noise, $n(t)$, from
an independent source with mean, m_N, variance, σ_N^2, and auto-correlation
function, $R_N(\tau)$, be added to the Class A and Class B waveform patterns,
generated by stationary Gaussian processes. The following question will
be discussed in this subsection: are the noise-corrupted patterns more
difficult to separate than the uncorrupted patterns? The result of adding
the noise is that a waveform, $v_i(t)$, generated by process no. i with mean
m_S, variance, σ_S^2, and auto-correlation function, $R_S(\tau)$, would seem to
have been generated by a new stationary Gaussian process (Middleton 1960,
Art. 7.5-1) with the mean, m_{S+N}, the variance, σ_{S+N}^2, and auto-correlation
function, $R_{S+N}(\tau)$. The subscript N refers to the word "noise". The subscript S refers to the word "signal".

$$m_{S+N} = E\{v(t) + n(t)\} \qquad\qquad\qquad ; (5.25)$$

$$m_{S+N} = m_S + \left(m_N\right) \qquad\qquad\qquad ; (5.26)$$

Due to the assumption of independence between $n(t)$ and $v_i(t)$, Equation
5.27 is readily obtained.

$$\sigma_{S+N}^2 = \sigma_S^2 + \sigma_N^2 \qquad\qquad\qquad ; (5.27)$$

$$R_{S+N}(\tau) = E\{(v(t) + n(t))(v(t+\tau) + n(t+\tau))\} \qquad\qquad ; (5.28)$$

$$R_{S+N}(\tau) = R_S(\tau) + \left(R_N(\tau) + 2\, m_S\, m_N\right) \qquad\qquad ; (5.29)$$

It will be noticed from Equation 5.26 and 5.29 that the effect of the noise is the addition of the terms in brackets. Recalling Equation 5.10, Equation 5.29 may be rewritten both in the form of Equation 5.30 and in the form of Equation 5.31.

$$R_{S+N}(\tau) = \left((m_S/\sigma_S + m_N/\sigma_S)^2/(1+(\sigma_N/\sigma_S)^2)\right.$$
$$+(\rho_S+\rho_N\cdot\ (\sigma_N/\sigma_S)^2)/(1+(\sigma_N/\sigma_S)^2))\cdot(\sigma_S{}^2+\sigma_N{}^2) \qquad ; (5.30)$$

$$R_{S+N}(\tau) = (m_{S+N}^2/\sigma_{S+N}^2 + \rho_{S+N})\cdot\sigma_{S+N}^2 \qquad\qquad ; (5.31)$$

Equation 5.32 shows the transformation that results from the addition of noise. Recalling Equations 5.26 and 5.27, Equation 5.32 may be obtained by first equating the two m/σ-terms and then equating the two ρ-terms in Equations 5.30 and 5.31.

$$
\left\{\begin{array}{c} \dfrac{m_{S+N}}{\sigma_{S+N}} \\[2em] \rho_{S+N} \end{array}\right\}
=
\left\{\begin{array}{c} \dfrac{m_N}{\sqrt{\sigma_S^2 + \sigma_N^2}} \\[2em] \dfrac{\rho_N}{1+\sigma_S^2/\sigma_N^2} \end{array}\right\}
+
\left[\begin{array}{cc} \dfrac{1}{\sqrt{1 + \sigma_N^2/\sigma_S^2}} & 0 \\[2em] 0 & \dfrac{1}{1+\sigma_N^2/\sigma_S^2} \end{array}\right]
\left\{\begin{array}{c} \dfrac{m_S}{\sigma_S} \\[2em] \rho_S \end{array}\right\}
\quad ; (5.32)
$$

It should be recalled that the values m_S, σ_S, and $R_S(\tau)$ only apply to the pattern $v_i(t)$, which was generated by process no. i. In the remaining part of this subsection it will be <u>assumed</u> that the AC power, σ_S^2, is the same for all uncorrupted waveform patterns. The transformation indicated by Equation 5.32 then becomes the same for all waveform patterns. The linear transformation simply consists of a scale change for both the m/σ- and the ρ-axis followed by a change of origin, and it gives a one-to-one correspondence between the $(m/\sigma, \rho(\tau))$-values before and after the noise addition.

Figure 5.3 illustrates the relation between two pairs of functions. The first pair of functions is

$$f_{1-D-1} = 2 \cdot h_1(m/\sigma, \rho) \quad \text{and} \quad f_{0-D-0} = 2 \cdot h_2(m/\sigma, \rho)$$

The functions h_1 and h_2 are the L-functions discussed in Subsection 5.3.3. The second pair of functions is

$$m/\sigma = h_3(f_{1-D-1}, f_{0-D-0}) \quad \text{and} \quad \rho = h_4(f_{1-D-1}, f_{0-D-0}).$$

The two pairs of functions represent a transformation and its inverse. Both pairs of functions have continuous partial derivatives of the first order, and the Jacobian (Papoulis 1965, Equation 7-35) is positive and non-zero for all values of the variables as may be seen from Figure 5.3; consequently, the figure illustrates a one-to-one mapping of points from the (f_{1-D-1}, f_{0-D-0})-plane over to the $(m/\sigma, \rho)$-plane and back. All points inside (outside) an arbitrary closed curve, F, in the (f_{1-D-1}, f_{0-D-0})-plane will be mapped into points which are located inside (outside a closed curve, M, in the $(m/\sigma, \rho)$-plane. Loosely speaking, the mapping consists of infinitely many local expansions and contractions of area, and no folding takes place. A sequence of three mappings will now be presented.

(1) Assume that the uncorrupted waveforms have been sampled and coded. Let the members of Class A and Class B be separable in terms of frequencies of certain pairs of delayed digrams with the same delay, e.g., f_{1-5-1}, f_{0-5-0}, f_{1-8-1}, f_{0-8-0}, etc. The i'th delay will be called D_i. The space where the set of attribute values are co-ordinates is called f-space. Due to the separability assumption some closed surfaces, f_{S1}, f_{S2}, etc. may be determined in the f-space, which together contain all members of Class A and no members of Class B.

(2) By repeated application of Figure 5.3, the pair of co-ordinates $(f_{1-D_1-1}, f_{0-D_1-0})$ is mapped into $(m_S/\sigma_S, \rho_{S,1})$, the pair of co-ordinates $(f_{1-D_2-1}, f_{0-D_2-0})$ is mapped into $(m_S/\sigma_S, \rho_{S,2})$ etc. In this manner any point in the f-space can be mapped into a point in a $(m_S/\sigma_S, \rho_{S,1}, \rho_{S,2}, \text{etc.})$ -space called S-space. During the mapping the closed surfaces remain closed, and the points inside (outside) a closed surface remain inside (outside). The members of Class A and Class B remain separable in S-space if they were separable in f-space.

(3) By repeated use of Equation 5.32, any point in S-space may be mapped into a point in $(m_{S+N}/\sigma_{S+N}, \rho_{S+N,1}, \rho_{S+N,2}$, etc.)-space called (S+N)-space by a linear transformation. The members of Class A and Class B remain separable in (S+N)-space if they were separable in f-space.

(4) By repeated application of Figure 5.3, any point in (S+N)-space may be mapped into a point in f'-space where the co-ordinates are new values of the frequencies of the delayed digrams with the delays, D_i, which were introduced in Step no. 1. During the mapping the closed surfaces remain closed, and the points inside (outside) a closed surface remain inside

(outside). The members of Class A and Class B remain separable in f'-space if they were separable in f-space.

During the Steps no. 1 through 4 it was assumed that the closed surfaces separated Class A members perfectly from Class B members. However, similar mappings may be performed for any set of closed surfaces. The closed surfaces F_{S1}, F_{S2}, etc., could for instance separate 90% of the Class A members plus 5% of the Class B members from 10% of the Class A members plus 95% of the Class B members. In answer to the question posed in the second sentence of this subsection it can be said that under the stated assumptions (especially: σ_S^2 being constant for all waveform patterns) it is possible to separate a set of Class A and Class B patterns, which have been corrupted by noise, as accurately as the uncorrupted patterns could have been separated. Two things should be noticed, however. The "adequate length" of the records may increase after the noise corruption. Also the separation in f'-space after the noise addition may require a separation surface that is more complicated than the separation surface which was required in f-space before noise addition.

5.4.3 A Carrier Wave Modulated by a Gaussian Process.

Let a stationary Gaussian process generate a waveform, $v(t)$, of adequate length. The process has the mean $\underline{m=0}$, the variance σ^2, and the auto-correlation function $R(\tau) = \sigma^2 \cdot \rho(\tau)$. The waveform, $v(t)$, is modulated by a carrier of frequency $w_c/(2\pi)$. The modulated signal is called $y(t)$. Disregarding an arbitrary phase angle at t=0 it is seen that $y(t)=v(t)\cdot\sin w_c t$. Let $y(t)$ be impulse sampled at instants $t=n\cdot\pi/\omega$ where n is an integer, $0\leq n<\infty$, and π/ω is a constant much smaller than $1/w_c$, $\underline{w_c\pi/\omega<<1}$. The positive samples are coded as '1', and the non-positive samples are coded as '0'; the coding algorithm is called the "sign algorithm". The delayed digrams f'_{1-D-1} are computed for the binary sequence; the delays $D \cdot \pi/\omega, D=0, 1, 2$, etc., cover the range of interest which is usually restricted to a few times the correlation time. For reasons of symmetry $f'_1 = f'_0 = \frac{1}{2}$. If the unmodulated, zero-mean signal samples, $v(n\pi/\omega)$, had been coded a binary sequence would have been generated that could have been described by the delayed digram frequencies

$$f_{1-D-1} = f_{0-D-0}, \quad D = 0, 1, 2, \text{ etc.}$$

The question may now be asked: if the value of w_c/ω is known, is it then possible to recover the values $\rho(D\pi/\omega)$, $D=0, 1, 2$, etc., of the normalized auto-correlation function from f'_{1-D-1}? In the remaining part of this section it will be shown that the question may be answered in the affirmative when $\underline{w_c/\omega}$ is assumed irrational, or in practice when w_c/ω is the irreducible ratio between two integers where the denominator is a large number.

Consider the two variables $\sin(n w_c \pi/\omega)$ and $\sin((n+D) w_c \pi/\omega)$, where n is an integer, $0 \leq n < \infty$, and D is an integer and a constant. The angle $D w_c \pi/\omega$ is taken to fall in the range $\pi \geq D w_c \pi/\omega > -\pi$. If and only if w_c/ω is irrational, as was assumed, the angle $n w_c \pi/\omega$ will be evenly distributed over the range 0 to 2π as n covers the range 0 to ∞ (Niven 1956, Section 6.3). The joint probability of the two sine-functions both being positive is $(\pi - |D w_c \pi/\omega|)/(2\pi)$; this result is obtained by considering two mutually exclusive possibilities. (1) $D w_c \pi/\omega$ falls in the range 0 to π. Given that $\pi \geq D w_c \pi/\omega > 0$, the probability of $\sin(n w_c \pi/\omega)$ and $\sin((n+D) w_c \pi/\omega)$ both being positive is $(\pi - D w_c \pi/\omega)/(2\pi)$. (2) $D w_c \pi/\omega$ falls in the range $0 \geq D w_c \pi/\omega > -\pi$. The probability of both sine-functions being positive is in this case $(\pi + D w_c \pi/\omega)/(2\pi)$. In either case, after the absolute value sign is introduced, the probability may be written as $(\pi - |D w_c \pi/\omega|)/(2\pi)$. The joint probability of both sine-functions being negative is for reasons of symmetry the same as the probability of both being positive. If the two sine-functions are not both positive or both negative, they must be positive and negative or negative and positive. The last two possibilities occur with equal probability: $|Dw_c\pi/\omega|/(2\pi)$.

Recalling that:

$$y(n\pi/\omega) = v(n\pi/\omega) \cdot \sin(nw_c\pi/\omega), \qquad \text{and} \qquad ;(5.33)$$

$$y((n+D)\pi/\omega) = v((n+D)\pi/\omega) \cdot \sin((n+D)w_c\pi/\omega) \qquad ;(5.34)$$

it is seen that the joint probability of both $y(n\pi/\omega)$ and $y((n+D)\pi/\omega)$ being positive depends on the signs of $v(n\pi/\omega)$ and $v((n+D)\pi/\omega)$ as well as on the signs of $\sin(nw_c\pi/\omega)$ and $\sin((n+D)w_c\pi/\omega)$. The joint probability of the sine-functions having each of the four combinations, $(+,+)$, $(+,-)$, $(-,+)$, and $(-,-)$, was derived in the previous paragraph. The joint probability of both signal samples, $v(n\pi/\omega)$ and $v((n+D)\pi/\omega)$, having each of the four sign combinations is f_{1-D-1}, f_{1-D-0}, f_{0-D-1}, and f_{0-D-0}; the frequencies were introduced at the end of the first paragraph of this subsection. There are four sign combinations of $(v(n\pi/\omega), v((n+D)\pi/\omega))$ and $(\sin(nw_c\pi/\omega), \sin((n+D)w_c\pi/\omega))$ for which $y(n\pi/\omega)$ and $y((n+D)\pi/\omega)$ both are positive. The first combination is $(+,+)$, $(+,+)$, the second is $(-,-)$, $(-,-)$, the third is $(+,-)$, $(+,-)$, and the last is $(-,+)$, $(-,+)$. The probability , f'_{1-D-1}, of both $y(n\pi/\omega)$, and $y((n+D)\pi/\omega)$ being positive may consequently be expressed as the sum of four terms.

$$f'_{1-D-1} = f_{1-D-1} \cdot (\pi-|Dw_c\pi/\omega|)/(2\pi) + f_{0-D-0} \cdot (\pi-|Dw_c\pi/\omega|)/(2\pi)$$
$$+ f_{1-D-0} \cdot |Dw_c\pi/\omega|/(2\pi) + f_{0-D-1} \cdot |Dw_c\pi/\omega|/(2\pi) \qquad ;(5.35)$$

Due to the assumption of zero mean for the process, m=0, it is seen that: $f_{1-D-1} = f_{0-D-0} = \frac{1}{2} - f_{1-D-0} = \frac{1}{2} - f_{0-D-1}$. The value of f'_{1-D-1} may consequently be expressed by Equation 5.36.

$$f'_{1-D-1} = |Dw_c\pi/\omega|/(2\pi) + f_{1-D-1} \cdot (\pi-2|Dw_c\pi/\omega|)/\pi \qquad\qquad ; (5.36)$$

The above expression shows that if f'_{1-D-1} has been measured and if w_c/ω is known, f_{1-D-1} can be computed. The two delayed digrams $f_{1-D-1} = f_{0-D-0}$ in turn determine $\rho(D\pi/\omega)$ through the diagram in Figure 5.3. Thus, it has been demonstrated that points on the normalized auto-correlation function, $\rho(D\pi/\omega)$, can be determined from f'_{1-D-1}. This completes the answer to the problem posed in the beginning of the second paragraph of this subsection. Notice that Equation 5.36 shows that $f'_{1-D-1} = \frac{1}{4}$ when $|Dw_c\pi/\omega| = \pi/2$ independent of the value of f_{1-D-1}. The reason is that a $\pi/2$ phase difference results in a 50% probability of sign change for any member of a $(v(n\pi/\omega), v((n+D)\pi/\omega))$ sample pair during modulation; the signs of $(y(n\pi/\omega), y((n+D)\pi/\omega))$ will consequently with the same probability have any of the four combinations (+,+), (+,-), (-,+), and (-,-).

Equation 5.36 expresses a linear transformation consisting of a compression of the f_{1-D-1}-axis followed by a shift of the origin. Let all the Class A and Class B waveforms first be modulated by the same frequency, $w_c/(2\pi)$, (say at the output of a sensor) and later (in the PR) be sampled with the same rate, ω/π samples pr.sec. It is then seen that if the waveforms were separable in terms of their delayed digram frequencies before modulation, e.g., f_{1-D-1}, they will also be separable in terms of digrams with the same delays after modulation, e.g., f'_{1-D-1}. Separation will in both cases be achieved with a separation surface of the same functional form. A practical consequence of this observation should be mentioned. If waveform patterns which are generated in a sensor by stationary, zero-mean Gaussian processes are modulated before they are sent to a PR, there is no reason to demodulate the patterns upon arrival if it is intended to code the patterns according to the "sign algorithm". Similar results will be obtained with the PR whether the modulated or demodulated patterns are coded according to the "sign algorithm".

5.5   The ρ_0 and ρ_m Concepts.

In this section first a few relationships will be reviewed which are valid for waveforms generated by a band-limited, stationary, random process; secondly, it will be shown how certain process parameters are related to binary word frequencies. Let $v(t)$ be a waveform generated by a band-limited, stationary, random process, and let it be assumed that the waveform record is of adequate length. The waveform will be assumed to have:

(1)   a power spectrum with average power M_0, a second order moment M_2, and a fourth order moment M_4;

(2)   an auto-correlation function $R(\tau)$ that has the second and fourth order derivatives $R''(\tau)$ and $R^4(\tau)$;

(3)   the average power $\overline{v(t)^2}$, it is also assumed that the time derivative of the waveform $v'(t)$ has the average power $\overline{v'(t)^2}$ and that the second derivative of the waveform, $v''(t)$, has the average power $\overline{v''(t)^2}$;

(4)   an average zero crossing rate of ρ_0; a zero crossing takes place whenever $v(t)$ changes sign;

(5)   an average rate of local extrema, local maxima and minima, equal to ρ_m.

The following relationships may then be demonstrated:

$$(2\pi)^2 \; M_2/M_0 \;\; = \;\; -R''(0)/R(0) \;\; = \;\; \overline{v'(t)^2}/\overline{v(t)^2} \;\; = \;\; (\rho_0/k_0)^2$$

$$(2\pi)^2 \; M_4/M_2 \;\; = \;\; -R^4(0)/R''(0) \;\; = \;\; \overline{v''(t)^2}/\overline{v'(t)^2} \;\; = \;\; (\rho_m/k_m)^2$$

k_0 and k_m are characteristic constants of the normalized, bivariate probability density function for the two variables $v(t)$ and $v'(t)$. If $v(t)$ is generated by a stationary Gaussian process or if $v(t)$ is a sinewave, $v(t)$ = $A\sin 2\pi ft$, k_0 and k_m may be computed; in both cases $k_0 = k_m = 1/\pi$ (Chang et al. 1951).

Let $v(t)$ be sampled and coded according to the following algorithm: "sample $v(t)$ at all local maxima and minima, and code all positive samples by a logic '1' and all non-positive samples by a logic '0'". Notice that the sampling rate is not constant with this algorithm. It is then seen that:

$$\rho_m \;\; = \;\; (f_{11} + f_{01} + f_{10} + f_{00}) \cdot (\text{Number of Samples per Second})$$

The result is obvious because the sum of the four digrams is unity. Whenever a '0' is followed by a '1' or a '1' by a '0' in the string of binits a zero-crossing has taken place. The axis is crossed approximately the same number of times in either direction (the difference is +1, 0, or -1) so it will be assumed (as in Subsection 3.2.2) that $f_{10} = f_{01}$. Recalling the definition of ρ_0, it is seen that:

$$\rho_0 \;\; = \;\; (f_{01} + f_{10}) \cdot (\text{Number of Samples per Second})$$

The number of samples/second equals the number of binits/second which again equals (the number of digrams+1)/second. Disregarding the constant, +1, the number of samples/second equals the number of digrams/second. A product like "f_{01}·(Number of Samples per Second)" simply becomes "the number of '01'-digrams per second". The value of a quantity like "the number of '01'-digrams per second" is very simple to measure.

Consider the case where all the waveforms that are members of Class A and Class B have been generated by processes of the same nature and where the process model Z has parameters that are related to (1) the shape of the power spectrum as indicated by the moment ratios M_2/M_0 and M_4/M_2, or (2) the shape of the auto-correlation function near $\tau = 0$. If all the processes may be assumed to have the same(or approximately the same) values of k_0 and k_m the possibility should be considered of separating the members of the two classes in terms of the following three attributes: the number of '11'-, '01'-, and '00'-digrams per unit of time; if the PR later is realized in hardware such attribute values are simple to measure.

6. THE HEURISTIC SEARCH PROCEDURE

6.1 The Search Rule.

In Section 2.1, Step no. 8, and in Block no. 16, Figure 2.1, it was mentioned that a search for new and more promising attributes should be performed. That such new and better attributes may be found by an organized, economical, non-exhaustive search through a hierarchical structure is one of the interesting features of the FOBW-method. In general, such a search cannot be performed among pattern attributes used with other design methods. But when the FOBW-method is used, all attributes are similar in nature, they are frequencies of occurrence of binary words, and simple relationships become possible among the frequencies, as illustrated by Equations 3.4, 3.14, and 3.24.

Before it can be decided that one attribute is better than another, some yardstick must be established by which the value of an attribute can be measured. In this chapter all attributes are rated according to their value of the S-measure. In chapter 4 the plausibility of the following assumption was discussed: the better an attribute is for separating members of Class A from members of Class B, the higher its S-value will be and vice versa; the assumption will be used several times in this chapter.

In this chapter it is assumed that the number of representative samples M_{AD} and M_{BD} both are so large that the means and standard deviations for the normalized Class A and Class B sample distributions can be used instead of the means, a and b, and the standard deviations, σ_A and σ_B, of the two probability density functions without introducing any appreciable error; this assumption was discussed in the first paragraph of Section 4.2.

The search for new and better attributes is performed according to a rule that will be described shortly. First, the notation will be established. Let $\Psi(N+1)$ be an $(N+1)$-gram or a delayed $(N+1)$-gram as defined in Section 2.2, Step no. 8. If the j'th binit in $\Psi(N+1)$ is replaced by a "don't care" statement, an N-gram called $\Psi(N,j)$ with or without delays is obtained; the N-gram is said to be contained in the $(N+1)$-gram. $\Psi(N+1)$ contains $(N+1)$ N-grams: $\Psi(N,1)$, $\Psi(N,2)$, ..., $\Psi(N,N+1)$. Let it be assumed that (i) it has been observed by the designer that k of the N-grams of the form $\Psi(N,j)$ all have frequencies of occurrence with the two properties (1) and (2) listed below, and that (ii) it is unknown whether or not the remaining $(N+1-k)$ N-gram frequencies have the two properties (1) and (2).

(1) The frequencies, $f_{\Psi(N,j)}$, have relatively high and not too different values of the S-measure so that they have been used as attributes with a categorizer design as described in Step no. 6, Section 2.2, and indicated by Block no. 12, Figure 2.1. During the categorization all the frequencies were found to be useful attributes as described in Section 2.5.

(2) The difference between the mean, a, of the M_{AD} $f_{\Psi(N,j)}$-values for Class A members, and the mean, b, of the M_{BD} values for Class B members, has the sign sgn(a-b); the second property is that sgn(a-b) is the same for all k N-gram frequencies.

The rule for searching for promising new attributes states that: <u>it is quite likely that $f_{\Psi(N+1)}$ will have a higher value of the S-measure</u>

than (i) any of the k frequencies of the form $f_{\psi(N,j)}$ and (ii) the average (N+1)-gram frequency. $f_{\psi(N+1)}$ should therefore be considered when the N_H attributes are selected for the next categorization attempt. The imprecise term "quite likely" is necessitated by the unknown factors, especially correlations which decide how useful $f_{\psi(N+1)}$ will be in the categorization.

The search procedure is heuristic in nature. There is no guarantee than all useful frequencies of (N+1)-grams may be found during the search. Some theoretical justification for the rule will, however, be given by way of two examples. An example with k=3 in Section 6.2 and an example with k=2 in Section 6.4 will be used to illustrate the search procedure and show why and how it works. The two examples should lend plausibility to the underlined statement above. A case study will be presented in Section 6.3.

The search rule makes it possible to use knowledge about N-gram frequencies to pinpoint a number of promising (N+1)-gram frequencies where an exhaustive search would have been uneconomical if not impossible. Also it will be noticed that the search procedure just described does not involve human judgement, it can be programmed for a digital computer.

6.2 First Example of the FOBW Search Procedure.

6.2.1 Three Digram Frequencies and One Trigram Frequency. Consider a pattern recognition problem where it can be <u>assumed</u> that $f_\psi = f_{\bar\psi}$ for all digrams and trigrams with and without delays as described in Section 3.7. Let it also be assumed that an attempt has been made to categorize the design data in Block no. 15, Figure 2.1, and that the separation was found "not acceptable". <u>Assume</u> that among the N_H attributes there were three delayed digram frequencies that:

(1) have delays D, E, and (D+E) sampling intervals, the third delay being the sum of the first two delays.

(2) all are contained in a delayed trigram with delays D, E; e.g., 1-D-0-E-1 contains three digrams: 1-D-0, 0-E-1, and 1-(D+E)-1.

(3) have differences between the Class A mean frequency, a, and the Class B mean frequency, b, of the same sign; sgn(a-b) should be the same for the 3 digram frequencies.

(4) have relatively high and not too different values of the S-measure.

In actual cases several sets of 3 such digrams can be expected to be discovered. In the remaining part of Section 6.2 the three digram frequencies f_{1-D-0}, f_{0-E-1}, and $f_{1-(D+E)-1}$ will be used to illustrate the search procedure. The values of the S-measure for the three frequencies are called S_E, S_D, and S_{D+E}. The value of the S-measure for the trigram frequency $f_{1-D-0-E-1}$ is called $S_{D,E}$. According to the first part of the underlined statement in Section 6.1 it is "quite likely" that $S_{D,E}$ has a higher value than either of the three digram S-measures. In the remaining part of this section it will under a mild assumption be examined when the "quite likely" event actually takes place.

6.2.2 Some Linear Relationships. For each sequence the four frequencies have a fixed, linear relationship as expressed by Equation 3.24. The Equation is repeated below:

$$f_{1-D-0-E-1} = (f_{1-D-0} + f_{0-E-1} + f_{1-(D+E)-1})/2 - \frac{1}{4} \qquad ; (3.24)$$

To facilitate the following computations an assumption will be made. It will be assumed that all three digram frequencies have the same value, s_A,

for the standard deviation, σ_A, for Class A members and that the three digram frequencies furthermore have the same value, s_B, for σ_B. The values
of s_A and s_B may or may not be different. The assumption will in a large
number of cases be in fair agreement with the experimental data. The trigram frequency standard deviation is called $s_{A,3}$ for the members of Class
A and $s_{B,3}$ for the members of Class B.

Equation 3.24 is valid for each of the members of Class A. The Equation is a linear expression in the four frequencies. By averaging over the
members of Class A Equation 6.1a is obtained; in the equation "a" is used
to indicate an expected frequency value for the members of Class A.

$$a_{1-D-0-E-1} = (a_{1-D-0} + a_{0-E-1} + a_{1-(D+E)-1})/2-\tfrac{1}{4} \qquad ; (6.1a)$$

Equation 6.1a relates the four mean frequencies. We are trying to find a
relationship among the four S-values; therefore, an equation is required
that relates s_A and $s_{A,3}$. For each of the M_{AD} Class A members of the design group an expression like Equation 3.24 is valid. Let (1) Equation
6.1a be subtracted from each of these M_{AD} expressions of the form of
Equation 3.24, (2) both sides be squared in each of the M_{AD} difference
equations, and (3) the average values for both sides be computed. The result is presented in Equation 6.2a.

$$s_{A,3}^2 = (3+2\alpha_{D,E} + 2\alpha_{D,D+E} + 2\alpha_{E,D+E}) \cdot s_A^2/4 \qquad ; (6.2a)$$

The three α-constants are the correlation coefficients. They are defined
by expressions like Equation 6.3a which defines $\alpha_{D,E}$. $E\{\cdot\}$ indicates the
operation of obtaining the expected value.

$$\alpha_{D,E} = E\{(f_{1-D-0} - a_{1-D-0})(f_{0-E-1} - a_{0-E-1})/s_A^2\} \qquad ; (6.3a)$$

Likewise let "b" be used to indicate a mean frequency value for the members of Class B. The following equation, Equation 6.1b, the equivalent of Equation 6.1a, may then be obtained.

$$b_{1-D-0-E-1} = (b_{1-D-0} + b_{0-E-1} + b_{1-(D+E)-1})/2-\frac{1}{4} \qquad ; (6.1b)$$

For each of the M_{BD} Class B members of the design group an expression like Equation 3.24 is valid. By the procedure described above, Equation 6.2b may be obtained. Equation 6.2b is similar to Equation 6.2a. Equation 6.2b relates $s_{B,3}$ and s_B. The three β-constants are the three correlation coefficients for Class B members. They are defined by expressions like Equation 6.3b which defines $\beta_{D,E}$.

$$s_{B,3}^2 = (3+2\beta_{D,E} + 2\beta_{D,D+E} + 2\beta_{E,D+E}) \cdot s_B^2/4 \qquad ; (6.2b)$$

$$\beta_{D,E} = E\{(f_{1-D-0} - b_{1-D-0})(f_{0-E-1} - b_{0-E-1})/s_B^2\} \qquad ; (6.3b)$$

It is now possible to find a relationship among the four S-values. When Equation 6.1b is subtracted from Equation 6.1a and both sides of the difference equation are divided by $(s_{A,3}+s_{B,3})$, Equation 6.4 is obtained.

$$S_{D,E} = \delta(S_D + S_E + S_{D+E})/2 \qquad ; (6.4)$$

The constant δ is defined by the following expression.

$$\delta = (s_A+s_B)/(s_{A,3}+s_{B,3}) \qquad ; (6.5)$$

6.2.3 Strongly Correlated and Uncorrelated Attributes. The two cases
$\delta = 2/3$ and $\delta = 2/\sqrt{3}$ will now be discussed.

(1) $\delta = 2/3$ results when there is maximum positive correlation among the
three digram frequencies, meaning that all α- and β-constants in Equations
6.3a and 6.3b are equal to +1. In this particular case where $s_{A,3}=3s_A/2$
and $s_{B,3}=3s_B/2$, the underlined statement from Section 6.1 does not hold
because $S_{D,E}$ is the average of S_D, S_E and S_{D+E} as indicated by Equation
6.6a.

$$S_{D,E} = (S_D + S_E + S_{D+E})/3 \qquad\qquad ; (6.6a)$$

$S_{D,E}$ can consequently not be larger than all three digram S-measures.
(2) Equations 6.2a and 6.2b show that when the correlations between the
digram frequencies decrease, the trigram frequency standard deviation becomes smaller compared to the digram frequency standard deviation; the
underlined statement from Section 6.1 becomes correct in more and more
cases. When all three digram frequencies are uncorrelated, all three α-
constants in Equation 6.2a and all three β-constants in Equation 6.2b are
zero. In this situation the relationships $s_{A,3} = \sqrt{3}s_A/2$ and $s_{B,3} = \sqrt{3}s_B/2$
are valid. This is the case where $\delta=2/\sqrt{3}$ and where Equation 6.6b obtained
from Equations 6.4 and 6.5 holds.

$$S_{D,E} = (S_D + S_E + S_{D+E})/ \sqrt{3} \qquad\qquad ; (6.6b)$$

Equation 6.6b shows that $S_{D,E}$ will have a higher value than any of the
three digram S-measures unless they have values that are quite dissimilar.
A high degree of dissimilarity is contrary to assumption (4) in Subsection

6.2.1. If the ratio between the three digram S-measures is $1/1(\sqrt{3}+1)$, $S_{D,E}$ is just equal to the largest of the three values. Consequently, when the largest of the three S-measures is less than $(\sqrt{3}+1)$ times the smallest S-measure it is certain that $S_{D,E}$ is larger than all three digram S-measures. The ratio $(\sqrt{3}+1)$ is larger than ratios usually encountered in realistic applications.

The following conclusion concerning the first part of the underlined statement in Section 6.1 can now be reached after the study of the cases $\delta=2/3$ and $\delta=2/\sqrt{3}$: as long as the three digram S-measures have similar values and the three digram frequencies are not strongly correlated it is quite likely under the stated assumptions that the trigram frequency will have a higher S-value than any of the three digram frequencies. It should be noticed that $f_{0-D-1-E-0}$ which is $f_{\overline{1-D-0-E-1}}$ is precisely as good an attribute as $f_{1-D-0-E-1}$. This is due to the assumption that $f_\psi = f_{\overline{\psi}}$. This assumption was introduced in the beginning of Subsection 6.2.1 so that Equation 3.24 could be used.

The following discussion is concerned with the last part of the underlined statement in Section 6.1. Let T_1 be a delayed trigram with delays D, E, and D+E selected in the manner just described and let T_2 be a delayed trigram picked at random among the unselected trigrams. T_2 contains three delayed digrams with delays F, G, and F+G and with S-values S_F, S_g, and S_{F+G}. It is the purpose of the following to examine the question: is f_{T_1} a better attribute than f_{T_2}? Let it be assumed that a relationship like the one from Equation 6.4 is valid in both cases.

$$S_{D,E} = \delta_{D,E}(S_D+S_E+S_{D+E})/2$$

$$S_{F,G} = \delta_{F,G}(S_F+S_G+S_{F+G})/2$$

T_2 is not a selected trigram so the following expression will almost always be true.

$$S_D + S_E + S_{D+E} > S_F + S_G + S_{F+G}$$

For certain unselected trigrams $\delta_{F,G}$ may be larger than $\delta_{D,E}$ but there is every reason to believe that $\delta_{F,G}$ on the average is larger than $\delta_{D,E}$. The expressions for $S_{D,E}$ and $S_{F,G}$ presented above do therefore indicate that $S_{D,E}$ is almost always larger than $S_{F,G}$. The larger value of the S-measure is taken to indicate that a delayed trigram selected after an organized search is a better attribute than one of the unselected delayed trigrams picked at random.

6.2.4 The Geometric Argument.   The underlined conclusion from Subsection 6.2.3 is also born out by the following geometric argument. Let a pattern be described by a point in three-dimensional (X,Y,Z)-space with the co-ordinates $(x_p, y_p, z_p) = (f_{1-D-0}, f_{0-E-1}, f_{1-(D+E)-1})$; such a point is called a pattern-point. The point is located inside a cube with side length $\frac{1}{2}$. The point has the distance θ_p to the plane with the equation $x+y+z = \frac{1}{2}$.

$$\theta_p = (x_p + y_p + z_p - \tfrac{1}{2})/\sqrt{3}$$

Equation 3.24 shows that $f_{1-D-0-E-1}$ has a simple geometrical meaning:

$$\theta_p = (2/\sqrt{3}) \cdot f_{1-D-0-E-1} \qquad \text{or} \qquad f_{1-D-0-E-1} = \sqrt{3}\theta_p/2$$

The pattern point is consequently located on the positive side of the plane. The normal to the plane x+y+z=½ through (0,0,0) will in this sub-section be called Θ. Each pattern point may be projected on the four lines: Θ and the three axis. Each of the projections corresponds to a reduction of decision space from three to one dimensions. The question to be ex-amined is if the projections on Θ will permit better separation of the Class A and Class B members than the projections on the X-, the Y- or the Z-axis. The assumptions which were made in the previous subsection are also made in this subsection. The S-measure associated with the projections on , the X-, the Y-, and the Z-axis are called $S_{D,E}$, S_D, S_E and S_{D+E}.

The points that illustrate members of Class A will have a centroid, M_A, determined be the three mean frequencies, $(a_{1-D-0}, a_{0-E-1}, a_{1-(D+E)-1})$. The centroid for Class B points is called M_B, it has the co-ordinates $(b_{1-D-0}, b_{0-E-1}, b_{1-(D+E)-1})$. Recalling assumption (3) in the beginning of Subsection 6.2.1 it is seen that:

$$sgn(a_{1-D-0} - b_{1-D-0}) = sgn(a_{0-E-1} - b_{0-E-1}) = sgn(a_{1-(D+E)-1} - b_{1-(D+E)-1})$$

The three mean value differences are proportional to S_D, S_E, and S_{D+E} with a factor of $1/(s_A + s_B)$.

The projections of M_A and M_B on Θ have the values $(2/\sqrt{3})a_{1-D-0-E-1}$ and $(2/\sqrt{3})b_{1-D-0-E-1}$. The eight mean values are subject to the following bond (obtained by subtracting Equation 6.1b from Equation 6.1a).

$$a_{1-D-0-E-1} - b_{1-D-0-E-1} = ((a_{1-D-0} - b_{1-D-0}) + (a_{0-E-1} - b_{0-E-1})$$
$$+ (a_{1-(D+E)-1} - b_{1-(D+E)-1}))/2$$

(1) In the case δ=2/3 all members of Class A are represented by pattern-

points located on one straight line, Λ_A, in space through M_A because all three α-coefficients (from Equation 6.3a) are +1. The line is parallel to Θ because all three standard deviations are assumed equal; they have the value s_A. All members of Class B are located on a (usually)different line, Λ_B, in space through M_B because all three β-coefficients are +1. Λ_B is also parallel to Θ; all three lines are parallel. Let the M_{AD} Class A points plus the M_{BD} Class B points be projected onto the three axes and onto Θ. In the case where Λ_A and Λ_B coincide all four projections obviously will give equally good separation, $S_{D,E} = S_D = S_E = S_{D+E}$. Let Λ_A and Λ_B slowly be moved away from each other while they are both kept parallel to Θ.A pencil sketch will now reveal that the projection of the pattern-points on one or maybe two of the axes will give better separation than the projection of the points on Θ. The same fact was expressed mathematically by Equation 6.6a.

(2)   In the case $\delta=2/\sqrt{3}$ the pattern-points representing members of Class A are distributed with their centroid at M_A. The variance is the same, s_A, for all three co-ordinates, and all three of the α-coefficients are zero. The points representing members of Class B are usually distributed in a different manner. They have their centroid at M_B. Let the M_{AD} plus M_{BD} points be projected onto the three axes and onto Θ as before. A pencil sketch will now reveal that the projection of the points on Θ will give better separation than any of the three projections on the axes as long as the difference in magnitude is not too great between $(a_{1-D-0} - b_{1-D-0})$, $(a_{0-E-1} - b_{0-E-1})$ and $(a_{1-(D+E)-1} - b_{1-(D+E)-1})$. The same result was presented in Equation 6.6b and the following material where it was pointed out that the critical ratio between the magnitudes is $1/1/(\sqrt{3}+1)$.

Notice that even when the trigram frequency is a better attribute

than either of the three digram frequencies, the trigram frequency alone
contains less information about class membership than the three digram
frequencies combined. The meaning of this statement in geometric terms is
that the co-ordinates of a point (x_p, y_p, z_p) determine the value θ of the
projection of the point on Θ, whereas the opposite usually is not true.

6.3 A Case Study.

6.3.1 Some Background Information.

It will now be described how in an
actual case it was possible to classify the members of three families using
only two attributes. The waveform patterns were generated by normal jet
engines and by two kinds of malfunctioning jet engines. All the records
were judged to be of adequate length by the method described in Subsection
5.3.5. Figure 6.1 illustrates in graphical form the mean frequency of
occurrence of the delayed digram 1-D-0, $2 \leqslant D \leqslant 50$ for the members of Class 1,
the members of Class 2, and the members of Class 3. In this application
as in many other practical cases it was found that each coded waveform
record contained approximately as many logic '1's as logic '0's. This
means that for all practical purposes $f_1 = f_0 = \frac{1}{2}$; consequently, knowledge of
f_{1-D-0} determines the remaining delayed digram frequencies.

$$f_{1-D-0} = f_{0-D-1} = \tfrac{1}{2} - f_{1-D-1} = \tfrac{1}{2} - f_{0-D-0}$$

The standard deviation for the Class 1 f_{1-D-0} digram frequencies is called
$\sigma_1(D)$. The standard deviations for Class 2 and Class 3 f_{1-D-0} digram frequencies are called $\sigma_2(D)$ and $\sigma_3(D)$. By inspection of the $3 \times (50-1)$ computed
standard deviations for f_{1-D-0}, $D = 2,3,\ldots,50$, it was found for all the 49

D-values that (1) $\sigma_1(D)$ had approximately the same value called σ_1, (2) $\sigma_2(D)$ had approximately the same value called σ_2, and (3) $\sigma_3(D)$ had approximately the same value called σ_3. There were minor differences among σ_1, σ_2, and σ_3. The S-measure has the values $S(D) = |a(D)-b(D)|/(\sigma_A+\sigma_B)$, where the subscripts A and B refer to any two of the three classes 1, 2, and 3. Based on this observation all values of the S-measure became proportional to the numerical value of the difference between the mean frequencies, $|a(D)-b(D)|$, as D covers the range D=2,3,...,49,50. Such differences are readily obtainable as ordinate-differences between curves in Figure 6.1.

6.3.2 The First Attribute. After a study of the 3 curves in Figure 6.1 it was decided first to perform the easier separation, the separation of members of Class 2 from the members of Classes 1 and 3. To simplify the hardware implementation it was decided to try to perform the separation with only one attribute. The first type of attribute that was considered was a delayed trigram frequency. The heuristic search that led to a useful attribute was performed in the following manner. An inspection of the 3 curves reveals that on an average members of Class 2 have relatively:

(1) low value of f_{1-13-0} compared to Class 1 members, and about the same f_{1-13-0} value as Class 3 members; the value of f_{1-13-0} is equal to the value of f_{0-13-1}, both being equal to f_1-f_{1-13-1}.

(2) high value of f_{1-27-0} compared to members of Classes 1 and 3; a high value of $f_{1-27-0} = f_{0-27-1}$ indicates a low value of f_{1-27-1} and of f_{0-27-0} because $f_{1-27-0} + f_{1-27-1} = \frac{1}{2} = f_{1-27-0} + f_{0-27-0}$.

(3) low value of f_{1-14-0} compared to members of Classes 1 and 3; the value of f_{1-14-0} is equal to the value of f_{0-14-1}.

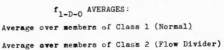

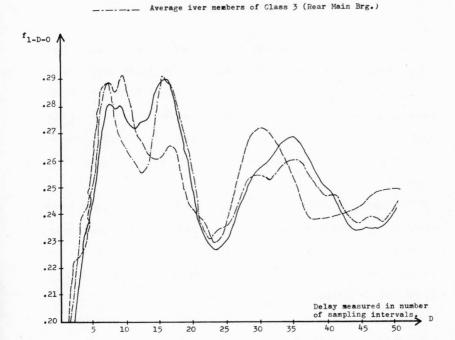

The delayed digram frequency f_{1-D-0} averaged over all members of Class 1, all members of Class 2, and all members of Class 3 for delays D, $2 \leq D \leq 50$. The diagram is used in Section 6.3.

Figure 6.1

The result of a heuristic search according to Section 6.1 is that the following four promising delayed trigrams can be constructed. The delayed trigrams contain the delayed digrams mentioned in Paragraphs (1), (2), and (3) above.

$$f_{1-13-0-14-1}, \quad f_{1-14-0-13-1}, \quad f_{0-13-1-14-0}, \quad \text{and} \quad f_{0-14-1-13-0}.$$

An actual test with the members of Classes 1, 2 and 3 showed that a better than 99% separation could be obtained with the decision rule: if $f_{1-13-0-14-1}$ is less than 0.145 the pattern belongs to Class 2, otherwise the pattern belongs to Class 1 or Class 3. The heuristic search method seems to offer useful results and substantially better economy than a blind systematic examination of delayed trigram frequencies with delays D and E, $2 \leq (D+E) \leq 50$.

The number of trigrams with delays D and E, $2 \leq (D+E) \leq 50$, may be computed in the following manner. There are $1+2+3+...+49 = 1225$ possible pairs of delays D and E, $2 \leq (D+E) \leq 50$. With each pair of delays eight, 2^3, trigrams are possible. The numbers of delayed trigrams that have delays D and E, $2 \leq (D+E) \leq 50$, is consequently $1225 \cdot 2^3 = 9800$.

6.3.3 The Second Attribute. The second and remaining step in the categorization procedure was to separate members of Class 1 from members of Class 3. To simplify the hardware implementation it was decided to try to use only one attribute. The search for a useful attribute was performed in the following manner. An inspection of Figure 6.1 reveals that on the average members of Class 1 have, compared to members of Class 3, relatively: (1) low values of f_{1-3-0}, f_{1-4-0}, and f_{1-7-0}; consequently, the values of

f_{0-3-1}, f_{0-4-1}, and f_{0-7-1} will also be low.

(2) high values of f_{1-10-0} and f_{1-11-0}; consequently, the values of $f_{1-10-1} = f_{0-10-0}$ and $f_{1-11-1} = f_{0-11-0}$ will be low.

(3) similar values for f_{1-14-0}, meaning that the values for f_{0-14-1} also are similar.

First a number of trigrams were constructed, the frequencies of which constituted promising attributes. None of these attributes separated sufficiently well although partial success was obtained by using $f_{0-3-1-7-0}$. Based on the trigram frequency, and (1), (2), and (3) above it was decided to try the promising delayed tetragram $f_{0-3-1-7-0-4-1}$. A test with the data showed that satisfactory separation, less than 5% error, was obtained with the decision rule: if a pattern belongs to Class 1 or Class 3 and has a $f_{0-3-1-7-0-4-1}$ value less than 0.058, it belongs to Class 1, otherwise the pattern belongs to Class 3.

The economy of the heuristic search procedure will be appreciated when the number of possible tetragrams with delays D, E, and F, $3 \leq D+E+F \leq 50$, are considered. E.g., if the first and last binit of a tetragram are separated by 6 sampling intervals the two binits in the middle can be located in $(6-1)(6-2)/2 = 10$ different ways, and for each of the resulting 10 sets of (D, E, F)-values there are 2^4 possible tetragrams. The total number of tetragrams spanning 6 sampling intervals is, therefore, $10 \cdot 16 = 160$. By generalizing from this example, it is readily seen that the number of possible tetragrams with $3 \leq D+E+F \leq 50$ is:

$$2^4 \cdot \sum_{n=3}^{50} (n-1)(n-2)/2 = 2^3 \cdot \sum_{(n-1)=2}^{49} ((n-1)^2 - (n-1)) =$$

$$2^3 \cdot (2 \cdot 49)(2 \cdot 49+1)(2 \cdot 49+2)/24 - 2^3 \cdot 49 \cdot 50/2 = 313600 \cong 3 \cdot 10^5$$

It would be highly impractical if not impossible to examine such numbers of frequencies during the design of a PR.

6.4 Second Example of The FOBW Search Procedure.

6.4.1 Two N-Gram Frequencies and One (N+1)-Gram Frequency.

In this example of the FOBW search procedure, the following problem is studied: when the two N-gram frequencies, $f_{X_1 X_2 \ldots X_N}$ and $f_{X_2 X_3 \ldots X_N X_{N+1}}$ both have the properties (1) and (2) mentioned in Section 6.1, is it then "quite likely" that the (N+1)-gram frequency, $f_{X_1 X_2 \ldots X_N X_{N+1}}$, has a higher value of the S-measure than both N-gram frequencies as claimed in the underlined statement in Section 6.1? X_1, $X_2, \ldots X_N$ and X_{N+1} are N+1 binary digits. For N=4 the three binary words can be illustrated by Figure 2.2 in the following manner. The tetragram $X_1 X_2 X_3 X_4$ is encircled and connected to a rectangle containing the pentagram $X_1 X_2 X_3 X_4 X_5$; the rectangle is connected to two circles, one of which contains the tetragram $X_2 X_3 X_4 X_5$.

The question that was asked in the previous paragraph will be answered by taking three steps. First, in Subsection 6.4.5 it will be shown that it is quite likely that either one or both of the two attributes $f_{X_1 \ldots X_N 0}$ and $f_{X_1 \ldots X_N 1}$, has a higher value of the S-measure than $f_{X_1 \ldots X_N}$. Secondly, in Subsection 6.4.6 it will be shown that it is also quite likely that either $f_{0 X_2 \ldots X_{N+1}}$ or $f_{1 X_2 \ldots X_{N+1}}$ has a higher value of the S-measure than $f_{X_2 \ldots X_{N+1}}$. Finally, it will be shown in Subsection 6.4.7 how these two observations lead to an affirmative answer to the question posed in the first sentence of this subsection.

6.4.2 Correlation Between N-Gram Frequencies.

Let $\Psi 0$ and $\Psi 1$ be the two

(N+1)-grams that are obtained by adding a '0' or a '1' to the N-gram ψ. The three binary word frequencies have the relationship expressed by Equation 6.7 for any member of Class A and Class B. It is as usual assumed that any member of Class A or Class B is a binary sequence of adequate length as discussed in Section 3.1.

$$f_\psi = f_{\psi 0} + f_{\psi 1} \qquad\qquad ; (6.7)$$

For each pattern record $(f_{\psi 0}, f_{\psi 1})$ is plotted in a co-ordinate system as illustrated in Figure 6.2. When a $(f_{\psi 0}, f_{\psi 1})$ point is projected onto the 45^0-line, it will be noticed that the distance from the origin $(0,0)$ to the projection is $f_\psi/\sqrt{2}$ measured in the unit from the abscisse and ordinate axes.

Assume that f_ψ, $f_{\psi 0}$, and $f_{\psi 1}$ have been measured for each of the Class A and Class B binary sequences and that each sequence has been represented by a pattern-point in the $(f_{\psi 0}, f_{\psi 1})$ co-ordinate system. Let the mean values of the three frequencies for members of Class A be a_ψ, $a_{\psi 0}$, and $a_{\psi 1}$. If so, Equation 6.8 is valid for each member of Class A.

$$(f_\psi - a_\psi) = (f_{\psi 0} - a_{\psi 0}) + (f_{\psi 1} - a_{\psi 1}) \qquad\qquad ; (6.8)$$

The standard deviations for the f_ψ, $f_{\psi 1}$, and $f_{\psi 0}$ values for Class A members are called s_ψ, $s_{\psi 1}$, and $s_{\psi 0}$. It will be assumed that M_{AD} and M_{BD} are so large that the first two moments of each sample distribution can be equated to their expected values without the introduction of any appreciable error. The variances associated with the estimates are given by Equations 4.4 and 4.6. The correlation between $f_{\psi 0}$ and $f_{\psi 1}$ values is determined by the coefficient r which applies to Class A members' frequency values; r is defined by the following expression. $E\{\cdot\}$ indicates the operation of obtaining the expected value.

$$r = E\{(f_{\psi 0} - a_{\psi 0})(f_{\psi 1} - a_{\psi 1})/(s_{\psi 0} \cdot s_{\psi 1})\}$$

By squaring Equation 6.8 and averaging over all members of Class A, Equation 6.9 is obtained.

$$s_{\psi}^2 = s_{\psi 1}^2 + s_{\psi 0}^2 + 2rs_{\psi 0}s_{\psi 1} \qquad ; (6.9)$$

Let α and β be defined by Equations 6.10 and 6.11.

$$\alpha = s_{\psi 0}/s_{\psi} \qquad ; (6.10)$$

$$\beta = s_{\psi 1}/s_{\psi} \qquad ; (6.11)$$

Equation 6.9 may then be rewritten as Equation 6.12 when $s_{\psi} > 0$. s_{ψ} is always greater than zero in practice because the M_{AD} sequences do not all have precisely the same f_{ψ} value.

$$1 = \alpha^2 + \beta^2 + 2r\alpha\beta \qquad ; (6.12)$$

Now the <u>assumption</u> will be made that the standard deviations for the f_{ψ}, $f_{\psi 1}$, and $f_{\psi 0}$ values for Class B members are proportional to s_{ψ}, $s_{\psi 1}$, and $s_{\psi 0}$. The Class B values are assumed to be K_B times as large as the Class A values, $K_B > 0$. The assumption is often satisfied in practice; its

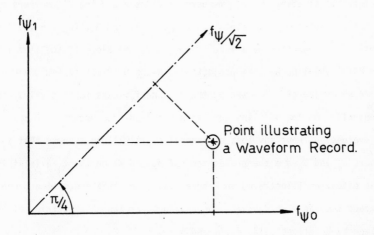

The Coordinate System with f_ψ, $f_{\psi 0}$, and $f_{\psi 1}$ axes discussed in Subsection 6.4.2. The unit for the f_ψ-axis is $1/\sqrt{2}$ as long as the unit for the $f_{\psi 1}$-axis or the $f_{\psi 0}$-axis.

Figure 6.2

meaning is readily explained when the standard deviation is regarded as a measure of the spread of the class members' frequency values around the mean frequency. The assumption states that if, as in Figure 6.3, the spread of the Class B members' f_ψ values around b_ψ is K_B times as large as the spread of the Class A members' f_ψ values around a_ψ , then the spreads of the Class B members' $f_{\psi 1}$ and $f_{\psi 0}$ values around $b_{\psi 1}$ and $b_{\psi 0}$ will also be K_B times as large as the corresponding values for Class A members. Under this assumption Equations 6.10, 6.11, and 6.12 reveal that the set of (α, β, r)-values is identical for the two pattern classes.

6.4.3 The Values of The S-Measure.

In Figure 6.3 the centroids for the points illustrating the M_{AD} members of Class A and the M_{BD} members of Class B are indicated by two points M_A, ($a_{\psi 0}$, $a_{\psi 1}$), and M_B, ($b_{\psi 0}$, $b_{\psi 1}$). The two points are connected by a line of length d, the slope of the line is $(\pi/4)+u$. The line has the projections, $d \cdot \cos u$, $d \cdot \cos (\pi/4+u)$, and $d \cdot \cos (\pi/4-u)$ on the 45° line and on the $f_{\psi 0}$ and $f_{\psi 1}$ axes respectively. The projection on the 45° line corresponds to a difference of $d \cdot \sqrt{2} \cdot \cos u$ in f_ψ-values. Without any loss of generality it will be assumed that $a_\psi \le b_\psi$ where a_ψ and b_ψ are the projections of M_A and M_B on the f_ψ-axis; this is the situation illustrated in Figure 6.3. Under this assumption u can never exceed the range $-\pi/2 \le u < \pi/2$. The S-values for the three attributes are given by Equations 6.13, 6.14, and 6.15.

$$S_\psi \quad = \quad |d \cdot \sqrt{2}\cos u|/(s_\psi + s_\psi \cdot K_B) \qquad\qquad ; (6.13)$$

$$S_{\psi 0} = \quad |d \cdot \cos (\pi/4 + u)|/(s_{\psi 0} + s_{\psi 0} \cdot K_B) \qquad\qquad ; (6.14)$$

$$S_{\psi 1} = \quad |d \cdot \cos (\pi/4 - u)|/(s_{\psi 1} + s_{\psi 1} \cdot K_B) \qquad\qquad ; (6.15)$$

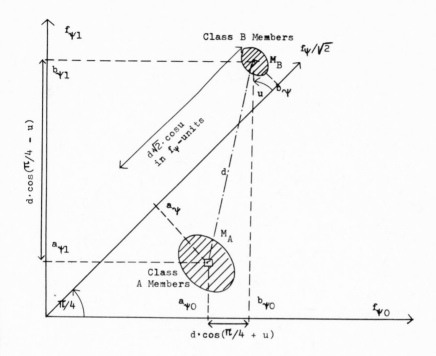

The diagram illustrates members of Classes A and B, in the manner described in Subsection 6.4.3. The Class A points have the centroid M_A, $(a_{\psi 0}, a_{\psi 1})$. The Class B points have the centroid M_B $(b_{\psi 0}, b_{\psi 1})$. M_A and M_B are connected by a line of length d with the slope $(\pi/4+u)$, $\pi/2 > u \geq -\pi/2$. The attributes $(f_\psi, f_{\psi 0}, f_{\psi 1})$ have the standard deviations $(s_\psi, s_{\psi 0}, s_{\psi 1})$ for Class A members and are assumed to have the standard deviations $(K_B \cdot s_\psi, K_B \cdot s_{\psi 0}, K_B \cdot s_{\psi 1})$ for Class B members. The correlation between $f_{\psi 0}$ and $f_{\psi 1}$ values is negative in the figure.

Figure 6.3

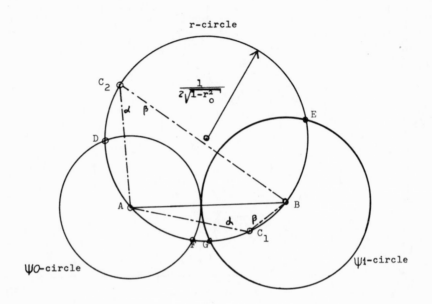

A geometric construction described in Subsection 6.4.4. The Chord AB is unity. r_0 is defined as $r_0=|r|$, $0 \leq r_0 < 1$. The shorter arc $\} AC_1B=Arc \cos(-r_0)$ is used for $r=r_0$. The longer arc $\} AC_2B=Arc \cos r_0$ is used for $r=-r_0$. The diagram illustrates the case where the radii of the $\psi0$-circle and the $\psi1$-circle both are less than unity meaning that $-\frac{\pi}{4}<u<\frac{\pi}{4}$. Points on the arc DAF illustrate situations where $f_{\psi0}$ is a better attribute than f_ψ. Points on the arc EBG illustrate situations where $f_{\psi1}$ is a better characteristic than f_ψ. The construction is valid for a particular value of u and r_0 and independent of d.

Figure 6.4

The question to be examined is: when does S_ψ satisfy one or both of the inequalities $S_{\psi 0} \geq S_\psi$, $S_{\psi 1} \geq S_\psi$? According to the underlined statement in Section 6.1 it is quite likely that either one or the other or both of the inequalities is satisfied.

Using Equations 6.10, 6.11, 6.13, 6.14, and 6.15, the two inequalities from the underlined question above may be rewritten as indicated below.

$$|\tfrac{1}{2} - \tfrac{1}{2} \tan u| > \alpha \qquad\qquad ; (6.16)$$

$$|\tfrac{1}{2} + \tfrac{1}{2} \tan u| > \beta \qquad\qquad ; (6.17)$$

The underlined question above is equivalent to the following question: under what circumstances are one or both of the Inequalities 6.16 and 6.17 satisfied? The question will be answered by a geometric argument in Section 6.4.4.

It is instructive to consider briefly the simple but non-trivial case where $\alpha = \beta = 1/\sqrt{2}$. This case is, for instance, encountered when the two cross-hatched areas in Figure 6.3 are two discs with uniform member-density and with (the same or) different diameters. It is readily seen from Inequalities 6.16 and 6.17 or from Figure 6.3 that in this case the underlined statement in Section 6.1 is true as long as u (which is located in the range $-\pi/2 \leq u < \pi/2$) does not fall in the range $-\pi/8 < u < \pi/8$. The range $(-\pi/8 | \pi/8)$ accounts for 25% of the range $(-\pi/2 | \pi/2)$. If all u-values are equiprobable, the underlined statement is true with probability 0.75.

6.4.4 A Geometric Construction. In this subsection it will be demonstrated through a geometric argument that it is "quite likely" that one or both of the Inequalities 6.16 and 6.17 are satisfied meaning that either $S_{\psi 0}$ or $S_{\psi 1}$ or both are larger than S_ψ.

Draw a circle, called the r-circle, with radius $1/(2\sin(\text{Arccos } r_0))$ where r_0 is a constant, $0 \leq r_0 < +1$. Locate a chord of unit length; the endpoints of the chord are called A and B as shown in Figures 6.4 and 6.5. Let C be a point on the shorter arc of the circle. For any location of C the angle ACB in the triangle, ABC has the value $\text{Arccos}(-r_0)$. The distances AC and BC have two equivalent relationships indicated by Equations 6.18 and 6.19.

$$1 = (AC)^2 + (BC)^2 - 2(AC)(BC) \cos(\text{Arccos}(-r_0)) \qquad ; (6.18)$$

$$1 = (AC)^2 + (BC)^2 + 2r_0 (AC)(BC) \qquad ; (6.19)$$

A comparison between Equations 6.19 and 6.12 shows that as C scans the shorter arc, (AC,BC) will take all the (α,β)-values possible for $r=r_0$. When C scans the longer arc (AC, BC) will take all the (α,β)-values possible for $r=-r_0$.

Draw a circle, called the $\psi 0$-circle, with radius $R_0 = |1-\tan u|/2$, and center at A, and a circle called the $\psi 1$-circle, with radius $R_1 = |1+\tan u|/2$, and center at B; u is an angle, located somewhere in the interval $-\pi/2 \leq u < \pi/2$. The two circles will always have one point in common. Whenever $-\pi/4 < u < \pi/4$, the sum of the radii is unity; the case is illustrated in Figure 6.4. The $\psi 0$-circle encloses the $\psi 1$-circle if $-\pi/4 > u \geq -\pi/2$; this is illustrated in Figure 6.5. The $\psi 1$-circle encloses the $\psi 0$-circle if $\pi/2 > u \geq \pi/4$.

If the point C falls inside the $\psi 0$-circle, Inequality 6.16 is satis-

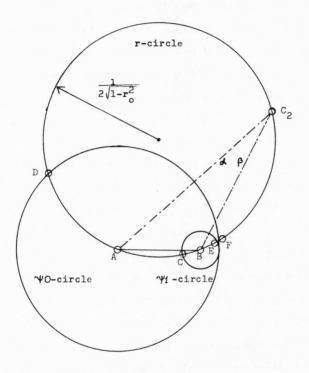

A second example of the construction described in Subsection 6.4.4. The case where $\pi/2 > u > \pi/4$ is illustrated. The $\Psi 0$-circle encloses the shorter AB-arc completely meaning that $f_{\Psi 0}$ is a better attribute than f_Ψ as long as the correlation between $f_{\Psi 0}$ and $f_{\Psi 1}$ is positive, $r = r_0$.

Figure 6.5

fied; the closer C is to the point A, the higher the value of $S_{\psi 0}$ is compared to the value of S_ψ. If the point C falls inside the $\psi 1$-circle, Inequality 6.17 is satisfied; the closer C is to the point B, the higher the value of $S_{\psi 1}$ is compared to the value of S_ψ. If the point C falls outside both circles, neither of the Inequalities 6.16 and 6.17 are satisfied. If C falls inside both circles, both inequalities are satisfied. Notice how all the important parameters have a one-to-one correspondence to specific parts of the geometric construction. r_0, the absolute value of r, the correlation coefficient, determines the radius of the r-circle. For positive r-values the shorter arc is used; for negative r-values the longer arc is used. Any point C on the periphery determines the two ratios between standard deviations $\alpha = s_{\psi 0}/s_\psi$ and $\beta = s_{\psi 1}/s_\psi$ as indicated by the Equations 6.12 and 6.19. The radii $|1-\tan u|/2$ and $|1+\tan u|/2$ are determined by the slope of the line which connects the points M_A and M_B in Figure 6.3.

It may be of interest to see the form the construction takes in the simple case that was discussed in the last paragraph of Section 6.4.3. Here $\alpha=\beta=1/\sqrt{2}$, which means that r=0 according to Equation 6.12. The r-circle consequently has radius $\frac{1}{2}$ and the situation may be illustrated by a point C_3 on the middle of one (say the lower) of the two half r-circles. When will C_3 fall inside the $\psi 0$-circle, or the $\psi 1$-circle, or both? This will happen if, and only if, one or both circles have radii larger than $\sqrt{2}/2$. Recalling that the radii are $|1-\tan u|/2$ and $|1+\tan u|/2$, $-\pi/2 \leq u < \pi/2$, it is readily seen that for $\pi/8 < u < \pi/2$ or $-\pi/8 > u \geq -\pi/2$ one or both of the circles will enclose the point C_3. This is, of course, the same result that was obtained in the last paragraph of Subsection 6.4.3.

6.4.5 Realistic Parameter Values. In this subsection it is discussed what values may be expected for the parameters, u, r,α and β. The values of the angle u can be expected to fall anywhere in the range $-\pi/2 \leq u < \pi/2$. The correlation between $f_{\psi 0}$ and $f_{\psi 1}$ is usually positive; this means that if a member of a class has a higher than average value of $f_{\psi 0}$, the same member can also be expected to have a higher (rather than a lower) than average value of $f_{\psi 1}$. The points which illustrate realistic cases may consequently be expected to fall on the shorter arc of the r-circle. For a typical value, r=$\frac{1}{2}$, the radius of the r-circle is $\sqrt{3}/3$, and the short arc is 120°. Usually $s_{\psi 0}$ and $s_{\psi 1}$ are of the same order of magnitude, meaning that α and β also are of the same order of magnitude; see Equations 6.10 and 6.11. The C-points which illustrate realistic cases will consequently be found near the midpoint of the shorter arc. E.g., points which are less than $\pm 30^{\circ}$ from the midpoint P_M of the 120° arc illustrate α/β ratios between:

$$\alpha/\beta = (1/\sqrt{2} - 1/\sqrt{6})/\sqrt{2/3} = 1/(\sqrt{3}+1) = 0.36 \qquad \text{, and}$$
$$\alpha/\beta = \sqrt{2/3} / (1/\sqrt{2} - 1/\sqrt{6}) = \sqrt{3}+1 = 2.73.$$

In practice $s_{\psi 0}/s_{\psi 1} = \alpha/\beta$ rarely falls outside the range 0.36 to 2.73.

It is instructive to follow what happens as u scans the range from 0 to $-\pi/2$. This operation corresponds to one quarter of a counter clockwise rotation of the line that connects M_A and M_B in Figure 6.3.

(i) $\underline{u = 0^{\circ}}$. The radii of the ψ0- and the ψ1-circles are called R_0 and R_1; they both have the length $\frac{1}{2}$. $2 \cdot \text{Arcsin}((1/4)/(\sqrt{3}/3))=51^{\circ}$ of the 120° -arc lie within the ψ0-circle, 51° of the arc does likewise lie within the ψ1-circle. Only points that are less than $\pm 9^{\circ}$ from P_M are not enclosed by either circle.

(ii) $\underline{0^{\circ} > u > -32.3^{\circ}}$. As u decreases from zero R_0 increases and R_1 decreases.

For u = -8.5°, tan u = $-2/\sqrt{3}+1$; consequently, the $\psi 0$-circle passes through P_M and encloses half of the points on the 120°-arc. For u = -32.3°, tan u = $-2\sqrt{2/3}+1$; consequently, all the points that are less than ±30° from P_M are enclosed by the $\psi 0$-circle; those are the points that represent realistic $s_{\psi 0}/s_{\psi 1}$ ratios.

(iii) -32.3°>u>-45°. As u decreases R_0 and R_1 continue to increase and decrease respectively. For u = -45°, (R_0, R_1) becomes (1,0) and the $\psi 0$-circle encloses all points on the 120°-arc; in Figure 6.3 the line that connects M_A and M_B is horizontal.

(iv) -45°>u>-65°. As u decreases both radii R_0 and R_1 become larger. For u = -65°, tan u = $-2/\sqrt{3}-1$, the $\psi 1$-circle passes through P_M and thus encloses half of the points on the 120° arc. For u = -52.5°, tan u = $-4/\sqrt{3}+1$, and the $\psi 0$-circle encloses all points on the r-circle.

(v) -65°>u>-72°. As u decreases both radii R_0 and R_1 become larger. For u = -69°, tan u = $-2\sqrt{2/3}-1$, and the $\psi 1$-circle encloses all points that are less than ±30° from P_M on the 120° arc. For u = -72°, tan u = -3, and the $\psi 1$-circle encloses all points on the 120° arc.

(vi) -72°>u≥-90°. As u decreases R_0 and R_1 both become larger. For u = -73°, tan u = $-4/\sqrt{3}-1$ now also the $\psi 1$-circle encloses all points on the r-circle. For u = -90°, the projections of M_A and M_B on the f_ψ-axis will coincide in Figure 6.3.

(vii) 90°>u>0. The discussion presented in the previous six paragraphs applies to the case where u scans the range 0<u<90° when the following modification is made: the notation (u, $\psi 0$, $\psi 1$, R_0, R_1) should be replaced by (-u, $\psi 1$, $\psi 0$, R_1, R_0).

The discussion above was concerned with a realistic case where it was assumed that r = $\frac{1}{2}$, and that actual $s_{\psi 0}/s_{\psi 1}$-ratios would be illustrated by points not too far from P_M on the 120°-arc. In the Paragraphs (i) through

(vi) the effects of u scanning the range $0 > u \geq -90^{\circ}$ were studied. It was demonstrated that the point P_M is enclosed by the $\psi 0$-circle for $-8.5^{\circ} > u \geq -90^{\circ}$ and by the $\psi 1$-circle for $-65^{\circ} > u \geq -90^{\circ}$. Consequently, if all u values are equiprobable, a point on the 120° arc near P_M will be enclosed (1) by the $\psi 0$-circle with 90% probability and also (2) by the $\psi 1$-circle with 28% probability.

It has been the purpose of this numerical example to lend plausibility to the statement from the second paragraph, Subsection 6.4.1: <u>it is quite likely that either $f_{\psi 0} = f_{X_1 \ldots X_N 0}$ or $f_{\psi 1} = f_{X_1 \ldots X_N 1}$ or both will have a higher value of the S-measure than $f_{\psi} = f_{X_1 \ldots X_N}$:</u>

<u>6.4.6 A Related Conclusion.</u> This far it has been demonstrated that under certain assumptions it is indeed quite likely that $f_{X_1 \ldots X_N 0}$ and/or $f_{X_1 \ldots X_N 1}$ is a better attribute than $f_{X_1 \ldots X_N}$ judging from the values of the S-measure. If Equation 6.20 rather than Equation 6.7 is used as the starting point, it may in a similar manner be demonstrated that it is also "quite likely" that $f_{1 X_1 \ldots X_N}$ and/or $f_{0 X_1 \ldots X_N}$ is a better attribute than $f_{X_1 \ldots X_N}$.

$$f_{\psi} = f_{0\psi} + f_{1\psi} \qquad\qquad ; \;(6.20)$$

It should be noticed that all the considerations in Subsections 6.4.4, 6.4.5, and 6.4.6 are independent of the value of d, the distance between M_A and M_B in Figure 6.3. The values of the S-measures are, however, proportional to d as indicated by Equations 6.13, 6.14, and 6.15. The observation that it is "quite likely" that $f_{\psi 0}$ or $f_{\psi 1}$ is a better attribute than f is consequently valid no matter whether the three S-values are large or small.

6.4.7 An (N+1)-Gram Frequency Suggested by Two N-Gram Frequencies. In this subsection it is shown how the results from Subsections 6.4.5 and 6.4.6 lead to an affirmative answer to the question posed in the first sentence of Subsection 6.4.1. In the following paragraph arguments are used which are intuitively obvious; in the next paragraph a more formal discussion is presented.

The (N+1)-gram $X_1 \ldots X_{N+1}$, is said to contain the two N-grams $X_1 \ldots X_N$ and $X_2 \ldots X_{N+1}$. Let the values of the S-measure for $f_{X_1 \ldots X_N}$, $f_{X_2 \ldots X_{N+1}}$, and $f_{X_1 \ldots X_{N+1}}$ be called $S_{1,N}$, $S_{2,N+1}$, and $S_{1,N+1}$ respectively. It has been demonstrated that it is "quite likely" that (i) $S_{1,N+1}$ is larger than $S_{1,N}$ when $S_{2,N+1}$ is <u>unknown</u> (Subsection 6.4.5) and (ii) $S_{1,N+1}$ is larger than $S_{2,N+1}$ when $S_{1,N}$ is <u>unknown</u> (Subsection 6.4.6). Consider the case where (a) $S_{1,N}$ and $S_{2,N+1}$ are approximately equal and <u>both</u> larger than the average S-values for $f_{X_1 \ldots X_N}$ and $f_{X_2 \ldots X_{N+1}}$ and where (b) the mean frequency differences have the same sign, signum$\{a_{X_1 \ldots X_N} - b_{X_1 \ldots X_N}\}$ = signum $\{a_{X_2 \ldots X_{N+1}} - b_{X_2 \ldots X_{N+1}}\}$; the Properties (a) and (b) are equivalent to the Properties (1) and (2) from Section 6.1. In cases which have the Properties (a) and (b) it is seen that the attribute $f_{X_1 \ldots X_{N+1}}$ is suggested by <u>two</u> (though related) N-gram frequencies rather than one N-gram frequency as in Subsections 6.4.5 or 6.4.6. Therefore, two statements are intuitively obvious. First statement: it is "quite likely" (if not more than "quite likely") that $S_{1,N} < S_{1,N+1} > S_{2,N+1}$ just as it was stated in Part (i) of the underlined search rule, Section 6.1. Second statement: it is unlikely that a (N+1)-gram which contains two N-grams with low or medium S-values should have an S-value higher than that of a (N+1)-gram which contains two N-grams with relatively high S-values; in general it may therefore reasonable be assumed that the (N+1)-gram frequencies that are selected by the search procedure are better attributes than the (N+1)-gram frequencies that are not so selected, or the (N+1)-gram frequencies which could have been picked at random. The second statement is equivalent to Part (ii) of the underlined search rule, Section 6.1.

It is instructive to see precisely under what circumstances $S_{1,N} < S_{1,N+1} > S_{2,N+1}$. Let it be assumed that 2^{N+1} sets of $(S_{1,N}, S_{2,N+1}, S_{1,N+1})$ -values actually have been computed, one set for each (N+1)-gram. Each set of S-values may then be represented by a point, Q, in the first orthant of an (X,Y,Z)-coordinate system. Q has the coordinates $x = S_{1,N}$, $y = S_{2,N+1}$ and $z = S_{1,N+1}$. The Q-points are assumed distributed according to a continuous, trivariate probability density function, $P(x,y,z)$. The centroid for the Q-points is called Q_m; Q_m has the coordinates (x_m, y_m, z_m). Now some properties of $P(x,y,z)$ will be discussed. (A) The only difference between $S_{1,N}$ and $S_{2,N+1}$ with regard to $S_{1,N+1}$ has to do with the direction in which time flows. The two directions cannot be expected on the average to give different (x,y,z)-values so $P(x,y,z)$ must be symmetrical with respect to the plane x=y; the plane contains Q_m, $x_m=y_m$. (B) $P(x,y,z)$ has the marginal probability density function $P_y = P_y(x,z)$ defined by Equation 6.21.

$$P_y(x,z) = {_0}\!\int^\infty P(x,y,z)dy \qquad\qquad\qquad ; (6.21)$$

The last two paragraphs in Subsection 6.4.5 indicate that the (x,z)-points (which are projections of the Q-points in the direction of the Y-axis) tend to fall above the line x=z in the (X,Z)-plane and to have positive correlation. (C) $P(x,y,z)$ does also have the marginal density function $P_x = P_x(y,z)$ defined by Equation 6.22.

$$P_x(y,z) = \int_0^\infty P(x,y,z)dx \qquad\qquad ; (6.22)$$

The (y,z)-points will tend to fall above the line $y=z$ and to have positive correlation. (D) It was assumed as part of Property (a) in the first paragraph of this subsection that $S_{1,N}$ and $S_{2,N+1}$ both be larger than the average S-value for N-grams. It is therefore only the space $(x>x_m, y>y_m, z>0)$ which is of interest. There is no indication that $P(x,y,z)$ should possess any particular features such as multimodality. It is in particular simple to see when the relations: $S_{1,N}<S_{1,N+1}>S_{2,N+1}$ are satisfied in the case where $P(x,y,z)$ in the region $(x>x_m, y>y_m, z>0)$ can be <u>approximated by a trivariate Gaussian distribution.</u> The Gaussian distribution will be symmetrical with respect to the plane $x=y$. For a given value of x called x_0, $x_0>x_m$, the associated values of z are represented by Q-points located in the plane $x=x_0$. The cut by the plane $x = x_0$ through $P(x,y,z)$ is illustrated in Figure 6.6. The line $y=x_0$ illustrates the intersection between the plane $x=x_0$ and the plane of symmetry $x=y$. As $x_0>x_m$ most of the Q-points will fall to the left of the line $y=y_0$. The loci for points with equal density of Q-points are ellipses, two of the equiprobability contours are illustrated in Figure 6.6; the density is highest at the point Q_0 with the coordinates (x_0, y_0^-, z_0). For reasons of symmetry and because $x_0>x_m$, Q_0 must fall on or to the left of the line $y=x_0$, $y_0<x_0$. Given $S_{1,N} = x_0$, the expected value of $S_{1,N+1}$ becomes z_0. As demonstrated in Subsection 6.4.5 it is quite likely that z_0 exceeds x_0 so Q_0 is located above the line $z=x_0$; in the fairly rare cases where $S_{1,N}>S_{1,N+1}$ the corresponding Q-points fall below the line $z=x_0$. z and y are positively correlated so the major axis for the ellipses will have positive slope. When it is known that $S_{2,N+1}$ has a value $y\cong x_0$, the expected value of z is defined by averaging over

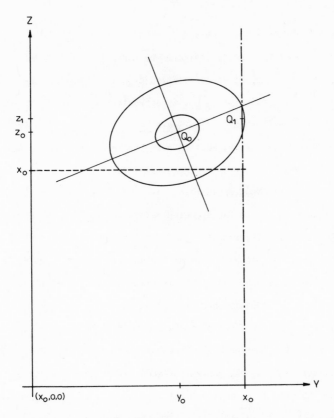

The figure shows a cut through a trivariate Gaussian distribution by the
plane $x=x_0$, $x_0 \geq x_m$ as discussed in the last part of Subsection 6.4.7.
The ellipses are curves through points with equal density of Q-points
(elliptical equiprobability contours). z_0 is the average z-value for
Q-points in the plane. z_1 is the average z-value for Q-points on the
line $y=x_0$. z_1 is larger than z_0, this indicates that $S_{1,N}<S_{1,N+1}>S_{2,N+1}$
with high probability.

Figure 6.6

Q-points located near the line $y=x_0$ (rather than over all Q-points in the quadrant); the mean value is indicated by the point Q_1 with the z-coordinate z_1. Due to the positive correlation $\underline{z_1\ \text{will exceed}\ z_0}$. The knowledge that not only $S_{1,N}$ but also $S_{2,N+1}$ is approximately equal to x_0 makes the "quite likely" event that $S_{1,N+1}>x_0$ $\underline{\text{even more likely}}$; this is Part (i) of the underlined search rule, Section 6.1. The relationship $S_{1,N}<S_{1,N+1}>S_{2,N+1}$ is satisfied when the corresponding Q-point falls above the line $z=x_0$ and near the line $y=x_0$. Now consider the case where the values of $S_{1,N}$ and $S_{2,N+1}$ are unknown; here the expected value of $S_{1,N+1}$ is z_m. However, due to the positive correlation it is seen that $z_1>(z_0>)z_m$, when it is known that $y\equiv x=x_0>x_m$; this is Part (ii) of the underlined search rule, Section 6.1. It has been assumed that the trivariate distribution $P(x,y,z)$ could be approximated by a Gaussian distribution in the space $(x>x_m,\ y>y_m,\ z>0)$. It will, however, be noticed that the argument just presented can be used as long as the loci for points with equal Q-point density, $P(x,y,z) =$ constant, are just smooth, convex surfaces rather than ellipsoids. As such distributions seem to be most natural it will be $\underline{\text{assumed}}$ in general that $z_1>x_0$ and that $z_1>z_m$ in accordance with the search rule.

   It has been the purpose of this second example in Section 6.4 to lend further plausibility to the search rule presented in Section 6.1.

7.   HARDWARE IMPLEMENTATION

7.1 Two Applications.

The FOBW technique can be applied to problems which are quite
different in nature. In this chapter two applications will be discussed:
detection of jet engine malfunctions which are manifest in the engine
sounds, (Page 1967), and recognition of the ten spoken digits. In the
first application, the signal to noise ratio is poor. The waveform
records, however, are much more than "adequately long" in the sense of
Section 3.1. In the second application the signal to noise ratio is good.
The changing statistics of the speech signal do, however, present some
problems which make this application most challenging.

7.2 Simple Hardware.

A salient feature of the FOBW method is that it gives rise to a
simple hardware design and realization. The basic hardware design is
shown in Figure 7.1. It should be noted that for various problems the
basic configuration may change somewhat in detail; e.g. the categorizer
may get its p inputs from several receptors in parallel each using a
different coding algorithm rather than just one receptor.

The signal conditioning block of Figure 7.1 may be as simple as an
amplifier or may contain many filtering and shaping networks. The sampling
intervals are determined either by a clock or by the signal itself. E.g.,

in the word recognition application the zero crossings of the waveform
derivative are used to trigger the sampler. The encoder consists of a
sampler and the implementation of an algorithm for the generation of a
binary pulse sequence. The binary sequence is fed to a shift register
where outputs from the various stages are connected to AND-gates. The
output from each gate indicates the absence or presence of a particular
binary word. When the output of the gate is counted or integrated in some
manner, the frequency of occurrence of the particular binary word may be
determined. Notice that many frequencies of occurrence may be determined
simultaneously (in parallel) using outputs from the same shift register.
This portion of the hardware composes the receptor. The categorizer is an
implementation of decision logic as discussed in Section 1.7; it may be a
simple form of threshold logic. These circuits with the inclusion of
additional timing circuits complete the hardware design in general. Circuit
design techniques have been used which enhance reliability (Becker 1961,
Becker and Warr 1963). To better appreciate the simplicity of the actual
design, the jet engine sonic analysis demonstrator has been treated in
some detail below.

7.3 The Sonic Analysis Demonstrator.

The Sonic Analysis Demonstrator, Figure 7.2, demonstrates the application of the FOBW technique to the problem of detecting jet engine malfunctions from the sounds generated by the jet engines (Page 1967). This
work was carried out under contract to and with assistance from the
General Electric Large Jet Engine Department. The demonstrator consists
of two parts which will now be described.

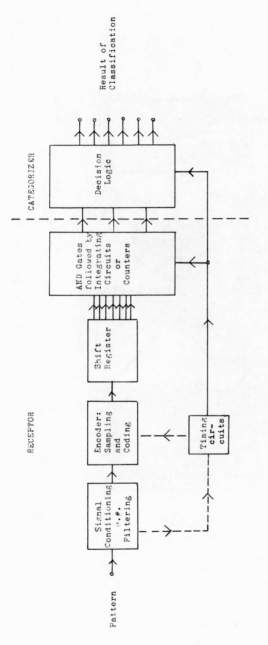

Basic hardware realization of FOBW
pattern recognizer, discussed in Section 7.2.

Figure 7.1.

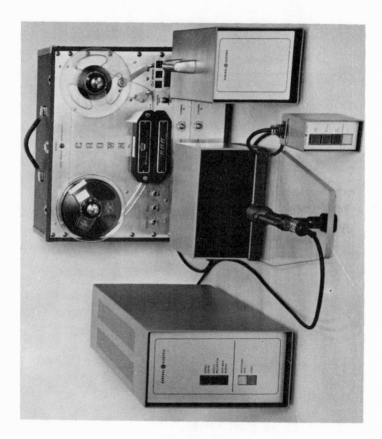

Sonic Analysis Demonstrator.
The PR is described in Section 7.3.
Figure 7.2

7.3.1 The Jet Engine Sound Simulator. This part generates jet engine
sounds in the following way. Using the same microphone position and an
idle speed of 3900 RPM, recordings were made of sounds from 2 normal J65
engines, A and B. Next, recordings were made of engine A with an installed
defective rear main bearing. Finally, recordings were made of engine B
with flow dividers bypassed; this makes engine B behave as if a nozzle
malfunction were present. 50 sec. were selected from each of the two malfunction run recordings and 25 sec. were selected from each of the normal
run recordings. The two 25 sec. recordings are repeated alternately on
track no. 1 of a four track tape. The 50 sec. recordings illustrating
rear main bearing trouble is repeated on track no. 2. The 50 sec. recording illustrating nozzle malfunctioning is repeated on track no. 3. Track
no. 4 was not used. The four track tape is mounted on the tape recorder
located in the background of Figure 7.2. In the foreground of Figure 7.2
a small box is seen with three buttons marked "Normal Engine", "Nozzle
Malfunction", and "Rear main Bearing", a fourth button is marked "Stop".
When one of the three buttons is pressed, the appropriate track is
played through the speaker shown in the center of Figure 7.2. In this
manner the jet engine sound generation is simulated. The box located to
the right in Figure 7.2 is the power amplifier for the speaker.

7.3.2 The Pattern Recognizer. The pattern recognizer consists of the
microphone plus the box located in the left side of Figure 7.2. The box
has one button marked "Start"; 6.7 seconds after the button has been
pressed one of the four lights on the box will be turned on to indicate
the decicion of the pattern recognizer. The lights are marked "Normal
Engine", "Nozzle Malfunction", "Rear Main Bearing", and "Insufficient

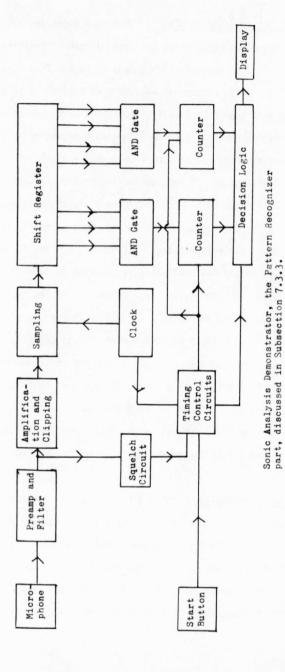

Sonic Analysis Demonstrator, the Pattern Recognizer
part, discussed in Subsection 7.3.3.

Figure 7.3.

Data". It should be emphasized that the only link between the simulator
and the pattern recognizer is the acoustical link between the speaker and
the microphone.

7.3.3 The Hardware Realization.

The hardware realization of the pattern
recognizer is simple and takes little room; the box to the left in Figure
7.2 is only 12" x 7" x 20". The block diagram for the recognizer is shown
in Figure 7.3; the diagram is a special case of the diagram in Figure
7.1. After the "Start"-button has been pressed, the recognizer will perform the following functions. The microphone output is amplified, filtered
and fed to a signal threshold circuit. The circuit performs the function
of amplification and clipping. In this manner the sign of the signal is
extracted continuously. The clipped signal is then gated by the clock in
order to produce a sequence of samples which represent the sign of the
analog input. By now the signal has been coded in accordance with the sign
algorithm from Step 2, Section 2.2. The binary sequence is fed to a 30
stage shift register where the presence or absence of two binary words is
detected by AND-gates in the two code logic blocks. In the learning phase
(Subsection 1.1.2), it was found that only two attributes were necessary to
provide the classification with the accuracy required; this matter has been
discussed in Section 6.3. The frequency of occurrence of the two binary
words is found by counting the number of times each of the words occurs during a fixed interval of time. At the end of the time interval the counters
are read out and compared to two thresholds. Based on the results of the
two comparisons, the decision logic circuitry decides which of the four
display lights should be turned on.

198

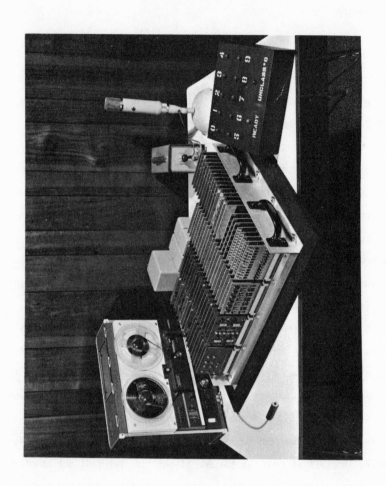

Word Recognizer.
The PR is described in Section 7.4.
Figure 7.4

7.4 The Word Recognizer.

Figure 7.4 shows a word recognizer which was built for the Apollo Support Department to demonstrate the FOBW technique (Becker et al. 1966). The machine can recognize the spoken digits from "Zero" through "Nine". The recognizer is so designed that its performance is reasonably independent of the speaker's sex and identity. Classification is achieved in real time by processing the speech data at the acousti- level only. A spoken digit is recognized if three constituent speech events of the spoken word are detected in the proper time sequence. Categorization of the different speech events in pattern space is accomplished by the instrumentation of six-dimensional orthopes (i.e., right parallelepipeds), in the space. The hardware implementation is totally solid state, portable, and consists of both discrete and integrated circuits.

The recognizer may be operated in one of two modes: The input signal can be either a microphone output generated by a speaker or a tape playback output generated by an audio tape with recordings of spoken digits.

8.   SUMMARY

It has been the purpose of this report to describe how frequencies
of occurrence of binary words may be used as attributes in pattern
recognizers. The description was presented in Section 2.2 in the form of
a nine step procedure, the FOBW procedure, illustrated by Figure 2.1.
Before the FOBW procedure was presented some problems in the design of
pattern recognizers were discussed in Chapter 1. The more important parts
of the FOBW procedure will now be briefly reviewed.

The patterns which are representative of members of Class 1, Class
2, etc. are converted into binary sequences by a suitable sampling and
coding algorithm. For reasons given in Subsection 1.7.4 it will suffice
to consider the case with only two classes, Class A and Class B. To keep
the presentation simple only waveform patterns are discussed, although
the FOBW method may be used with other kinds of patterns. Before a suitable sampling and coding algorithm can be selected, the designer must
model the random processes that generate the patterns; some examples of
algorithms that apply to important models are presented in Chapter 5.

The binary sequences are examined to find binary words which appear
significantly more often (or seldom) in coded Class A patterns than in
coded Class B patterns. The significance of each binary word frequency
difference is estimated by the S-measure; the S-measure is discussed in
Chapter 4. The binary word frequencies are ordered in an array according

to decreasing values of the S-measure as described in Section 2.3. The ordered array is the main design variable; after the array has been established all the following events in the PR design have largely been determined. Binary words are symmetrical or unsymmetrical. Frequencies of symmetrical binary words may contain information related to "amplitude information"; frequencies of unsymmetrical words may also contain information related to "phase information" as discussed in Section 3.8.

It is attempted to separate the two classes of coded patterns using the most effective set of N_H attributes from the array. One possible means for separation has been described in Section 2.5. Problems associated with decision making and categorizer design have been discussed in Sections 1.6 and 1.7. If the separation of the design data is satisfactory, the PR design is evaluated with the test data as discussed in Subsection 1.4.2; if the result is satisfactory, the PR is realized in hardware or software and the project is completed. If the separation of the design data or the test data is unsatisfactory, the design is improved by iteration.

It is one of the strong points of the FOBW procedure that the PR design may be improved in a systematic manner. The design through iterations may be performed by a program for a general purpose computer. During each iteration the attributes which seemed effective in the previous attempt to separate the design data are used in the search for new and promising attributes, frequencies of longer binary words. In Chapter 6 it is described how the search is performed and why the new attributes hold promise. The arguments in Chapter 6 are made possible by the computational rules derived in Chapter 3. The result of each iteration is that a new set of N_H attributes is generated as described in Section 2.4. The new set of attributes is used in a new attempt to separate the design data. If the attempt is successful, an improved PR design has been obtained which is used to separate the test data, etc., etc.

If an acceptable PR design is obtained after one or more iterations, the design is realized in hardware or software, as the case may be. When the FOBW method is used the hardware realization is inherently simple and reliable as discussed in Section 1.8 and Chapter 7.

Most of the new concepts in this report were developed to overcome particular practical problems; the author does therefore believe that many of the concepts can be extended, systemized and unified and he would be grateful for any suggestions the reader may have to offer.

The ideas which have been presented in this report are simple ideas; the author hopes that he succeeded in making them appear as such.

BIBLIOGRAPHY

Abend, K., Harley, T.J. and Kanal, L.N. (1965), "Classification of Binary Random Patterns", IEEE Trans. on Info. Theory, vol. IT-11, no. 4, pp. 538-544, Oct. 1965.

Abramowitz, M. and Stegun, I.A. (Edit.)(1964). "Handbook of Mathematical Functions". Washington, D.C.: Superintendent of Documents, 1964. Section 2.6.3.

Abramson, N. and Braverman, D. (1962), "Learning to Recognize Patterns in a Random Environment", IRE Trans. on Info. Theory, vol. IT-8, no. 5, pp. 58-63, Sep. 1962.

Akers, Jr., S.B. (1965), "Techniques of Adaptive Decision Making", TIS R65ELS-12 (Internal Publication, General Electric Company), 1965.

Akers, Jr., S.B. and Rutter, B.H. (1964), "The Use of Threshold Logic in Character Recognition", Proc. IEEE, vol. 52, no. 8, pp. 931-938, Aug. 1964.

Anderson, T.W. (1958), "An Introduction to Multivariate Statistical Analysis". New York: John Wiley and Sons, Inc., 1958.

Anderson, T.W. and Bahadur, R.R. (1962), "Classification into Two Multivariate Normal Distributions with Different Covariance Matrices", Annals of Mathematical Statistics, vol. 33, pp. 420-431, June 1962.

Anderson, W.W. (1965), "Optimum Estimation of the Mean of a Gaussian Process", Proc. IEEE. vol. 53, no. 10, pp. 1640-1641, Oct. 1965. (Correspondence).

Andrews, Harry C., Introduction to Mathematical Techniques in Pattern Recognition. New York: Wiley-Interscience, 1972.

Arley, N. and Buch, K.R. (1966), "Introduction to the Theory of Probability and Statistics", New York: Science Editions (Paperback edition), 1966.

Attneave, F. (1959), "Applications of Information Theory to Psychology". New York: Henry Holt and Co., 1959.

Bacon, R.H. (1963), "Approximations to Multivariate Normal Orthant Probabilities". Annals of Mathematical Statistics, vol. 34, no. 1, pp. 191-198, March 1963.

Bacus, J.W. and Gose, E.E. (1972), "Leukocyte Pattern Recognition". IEEE Trans. on Systems, Man, and Cybernetics, vol. SMC-2, no. 4, pp. 513-526, Sep. 1972.

Bajcsy and Tavakoli (1974), "Computer Recognition of Roads from Satellite Pictures". Paper in SIJCPR (1974).

Becker, P.W. (1961), "Static Design of Transistor Diode Logic", IRE Trans. on Circuit Theory, vol. CT-8, no. 4, pp. 461-467, Dec. 1961.

Becker P.W. (1966), "The Frequency of Binary Word Techniques for Recognition of Patterns". TIS R66ELS-28, (Internal Publication, General Electric Company), June 1966.

Becker, P.W. (1972), "An Introduction to the Design of Pattern Recognition Devices". Springer Verlag, New York-Wien, 1972. ISBN 0-387-81153-2.

Becker, P.W. (1974), "What Multivariate Probability Densities are possible with a Specified Set of Marginals?" Paper in SIJCPR (1974).

Becker, P.W., Haskin, L.B., Korzekwa, S.W. and Robbins, T.C. (1966), "A Pattern Recognizer for the Spoken Digits". TIS R66ELS-21, (Internal Publication, General Electric Company), May 1966.

Becker, P.W. and Jensen, F. (1974), "Design of Systems and Circuits for Maximum Reliability or Maximum Production Yield". Copenhagen: Den Private Ingeniørfond (1974).

Becker, P.W. and Nielsen, K.A. (1972), "Pattern Recognition Using Dynamic Pictorial Information". IEEE Trans. on Systems, Man, and Cybernetics, vol. SMC-2, no. 3, pp. 85-87, July 1972. Reprinted as Appendix 3 in Becker (1972).

Becker, P.W. and Thamdrup, J.E. (1972), "Pattern Recognition Applied to Automated Testing". IEE Conference Publication no. 91, pp. 82-86, Sep. 1972.

Becker, P.W. and Warr, R.E. (1963), "Reliability vs. Component Tolerances in Microelectronic Circuits". Proc. IEEE, vol. 51. no. 9, pp. 1202-1314, Sep. 1963.

Bell (1974), "Decision Trees Made Easy". Paper in SIJCPR (1974).

Blachmann, N.M. (1974), "Sinusoids vs. Walsh Functions". Proc. IEEE, vol. 62, no. 3, pp. 346-354, March 1974.

Bonner, R.E. (1964), "On Some Clustering Techniques", IBM Journal of R and D, vol. 8, no. 1, pp. 22-32, Jan. 1964.

Bonner, R.E. (1966), "Pattern Recognition with Three Added Requirements". IEEE Trans. on Electr. Comp., vol. EC-15, no. 5, pp. 770-781, Oct. 1966.

Booth, A.L. (1973), "Cloud Type Pattern Recognition Using Environmental Satellite Data". Paper in FIJCPR (1973).

Borriello, Caponetti, and Fusco (1974), "Urban Area Analysis by Multispectral Satellite's Images". Paper in SIJCPR (1974).

Brain, A.E., Hart, P.E. and Munson, J.H. (1966), "Graphical-Data-Processing Research Study and Experimental Investigation", Tech. Rept. ECOM-o1901-25, Stanford Research Inst., Menlo Park, Calif., Dec. 1966.

Bremermann, H.J. (1968), "Pattern Recognition, Functionals, and Entropy", IEEE Trans. on Bio-Medical Engineering, vol. BME-15, no. 3, pp. 201-207, July 1968.

Brick, D.B. (1968), "On the Applicability of Wiener's Canonical Expansions". IEEE Trans. on Systems, Science and Cybernetics, vol.SSC-4, no. 1, pp. 29-38, March 1968.

Caceres, Cesar A. and Dreifus, L.S. (1970), editors. "Clinical Electrocardiography and Compurters". New York: Academic Press, 1970.

Cardillo, G.P. and Fu, K.S. (1967), "Divergence and Linear Classifiers for Feature Selection", IEEE Trans. on Automatic Control, vol. AC-12, no. 6, pp. 780-781, Dec. 1967. (Correspondence).

Carlyle, J.W. and Thomas, J.B. (1964), "On Nonparametric Signal Detectors", IEEE Trans. on Info. Theory, vol. IT-10, no. 2, pp. 146-152, April 1964.

Carne, E.B. (1965), "Artificial Intelligence Techniques", Washington, D.C.: Spartan Division (Books, Inc.), 1965).

Casey, R.G. (1970), "Moment Normalization of Handprinted Characters". IBM Journal of Research and Development, vol. 14, no. 5, pp. 548-557, Sep. 1970.

Casparsson, T. and Zech, L. (1973), "Chromosome Identification". New York: Academic Press; published by the Nobel Foundation, Stockholm 1973.

Chang, S., Pihl, G.E. and Essigmann, M.W. (1951), "Representation of Speech Sounds and Some of Their Statistical Properties", Appendix, Proc. IRE, vol. 39, no. 2, pp. 147-153, Feb. 1951.

Chen, C.H. (1965), "A Computer Searching Criterion for Best Feature Set in Character Recognition", Proc. IEEE, vol. 53, no. 12, pp. 2128-2129, Dec. 1965. (Correspondence).

Chen, C.H. (1966), "A Note on a Sequential Decision Approach to Pattern Recognition and Machine Learning", Information and Control, vol. 9, no. 6, pp. 549-562, Dec. 1966.

Chen (1974), "Feature Extraction and Computational Complexity in Seismological Pattern Recognition". Paper in SIJCPR (1974).

Chernoff, H. (1970), "A Bound on the Classification Error for Discriminating Between Populations With Specified Means and Variances". Technical Report No. 66; Jan. 5, 1970; Dept. of Statistics, Stanford University, Calif.

Chien, Y.P. and Fu, K.S. (1974), "Recognition of X-Ray Picture Patterns", IEEE Trans. on Systems, Man, and Cybernetics, vol. SMC-4, no. 2, pp. 145-156, March 1974.

Chien, Y.T. and Fu, K.S. (1967a), "On Bayesian Learning and Stochastic Approximation", IEEE Trans. on Systems, Science and Cybernetics, vol. SSC-3, no. 1, pp. 28-38, June 1967.

Chien, Y.T. and Fu, K.S. (1967b), "On the Generalized Karhunen-Loéve Expansion", IEEE Trans. on Info. Theory, vol. IT-13, no. 3, pp. 518-520, July 1967. (Correspondence).

Chow, C.K. (1957), "An Optimum Character Recognition System Using Decision Functions", IRE Trans. on Electr. Comp., vol. EC-6, no. 4, pp. 247-254, Dec. 1957.

Chow, C.K. (1966), "A Class of Nonlinear Recognition Procedures", IEEE Trans. on Systems, Science and Cybernetics, vol. SSC-2, pp. 101-109, Dec. 1966.

Chow, C.K. (1970), "On Optimum Recognition Error and Reject Tradeoff", IEEE Trans. on Info. Theory, vol. IT-16, no. 1, pp. 41-46, Jan. 1970.

Clapper, G.L. (1971), "Automatic Word Recognition", IEEE Spectrum, vol. 8, no. 8, pp. 57-69, August 1971.

Cochran, W.T., Cooley, J.W., Favin, D.L., Helms, H.D., Kaenel, R.A., Lang, W.W., Maling, Jr., G.C., Nelson, D.E., Rader, C.M., and Welch, P.D. (1967), "What is the Fast Fourier Transform?" Proc. IEEE, vol. 55, no. 10, pp. 1664-1674, Oct. 1967.

Collins, N.L. and Michie, D. (1967), editors, "Machine Intelligence 1", London, U.K.: Oliver and Boyd Ltd., 1967.

Cooper, P.W. (1964), "Hyperplanes, Hyperspheres and Hyperquadrics as Decision Boundaries", in Tou and Wilcox 1964, pp. 111-138.

207

Cooper, D.B. and Cooper, P.W. (1964), "Non-supervised Adaptive Signal
Detection and Pattern Recognition", Information and Control,
vol. 7, no. 3, pp. 416-444, Sep. 1964.

Cox, J.R., Nolle, F.M. and Arthur, R.M. (1972), "Digital Analysis of
the Electroencephalogram, the Blood Pressure Wave, and the
Electrocardiogram". Proc. IEEE, vol. 60, no. 10, pp. 1137-1164,
Oct. 1972.

Dale, E. and Michie, D. (1968), editors, "Machine Intelligence 2",
London, U.K.: Oliver and Boyd Ltd., 1968.

Davenport, Jr., W.B. and Root, W.L. (1958), "An Introduction to the
Theory of Random Signals and Noise". New York: McGraw-Hill,
1958.

David, E.E. and Denes, P.B. (1972), "Human Communication: A Unified
View". New York: McGraw-Hill, 1972, Chapter 10.

Deutsch, Sid (1967), "Models of the Nervous System". New York: John
Wiley and Sons, Inc., 1967.

Duda, R.O. and Fossum, H. (1966), "Pattern Classification by Iterative-
ly Determined Linear and Piecewise Linear Discriminant
Functions". IEEE Trans. on Electr. Comp., vol. EC-15, no. 2,
pp. 220-232, April 1966.

Duda, R.O. and Hart, P.E. (1973), "Pattern Classification and Scene
Analysis". New York: Wiley-Interscience, 1973.

Eleccion, M. (1973), "Automatic Fingerprint Identification". IEEE
Spectrum, vol. 10, no. 9, pp. 36-45, Sep. 1973.

Fawe, A.L. (1966), "Interpretation of Infinitely Clipped Speech
Properties". IEEE Trans. on Audio and Electroacoustics,
vol. AU-14, no. 4, pp. 178-183, Dec. 1966.

Feigenbaum, E.A. and Feldman, J. (1963), editors, "Computers and
Thought". New York: McGraw-Hill, 1963.

Feth, G.C. (1973), "Memories are Bigger, Faster - and Cheaper".
IEEE Spectrum, vol. 10, no. 11, pp. 28-35, Nov. 1973.

FIJCPR (1973), "The Proceedings of the First International Joint
Conference on Pattern Recognition". Washington, D.C., 1973.
IEEE Catalog no. 73CHO 829-9C.

FIJCPR (1973), "CR II". The Session: Character Recognition II in
FIJCPR (1973).

Fine, T. and Johnson, N. (1965), "On the Estimation of the Mean of a
Random Process". Proc. IEEE, vol. 53, no. 2, pp. 187-188,
Feb. 1965 (Correspondence).

Firschein, O. and Fischler, M. (1963), "Automatic Subclass Determination for Pattern Recognition Applications". IEEE Trans. on Electr. Comp., vol. EC-12, no. 2, pp. 137-141, April 1963. (Correspondence).

Fisher, R.A. (1963), "Statistical Methods for Research Workers". 13th Edition, New York: Hafner, 1963.

Freedman, M.D. (1972), "Optical Character Recognition". IEEE Spectrum, vol. 11, no. 3, pp. 44-52, March 1972.

Freeman, H. and Garder, L. (1964), "Apictorial Jigsaw Puzzles: The Computer Solution of a Problem in Pattern Recognition". IEEE Trans. on Electr. Comp., vol. EC-13, no. 2, pp. 118-127, April 1964.

Fu, K.S. (1968), "Sequential Methods in Pattern Recognition and Machine Learning". New York: Academic Press, 1968.

Fu, K.S. (1974), "Syntactic Methods in Pattern Recognition". New York: Academic Press, 1974.

Fu, K.S. and Chien, Y.T. (1967a), "Sequential Recognition Using a Nonparametric Ranking Procedure". IEEE Trans. on Info. Theory, vol. IT-13, no. 3, July 1967.

Fu, K.S., Chien, Y.T. and Cardillo, G.P. (1967b), "A Dynamic Programming Approach to Sequential Pattern Recognition". IEEE Trans. on Electr. Comp., vol. EC-16, no. 6, pp. 790-803, Dec. 1967.

Glucksman, H.A. (1965), "A Parapropagation Pattern Classifier". IEEE Trans. on Electr. Comp., vol. EC-14, no. 3, pp. 434-443, June 1965.

Glucksman, H. (1966), "On the Improvement of a Linear Separation by Extending the Adaptive Process with a Stricter Criterion". IEEE Trans. on Electr. Comp., vol. EC-15, no. 6, pp. 941-944, Dec. 1966. (Short note).

Gold, B. (1959), "Machine Recognition of Hand-Sent Morse Code". IRE Trans. on Info. Theory, vol. IT-5, no. 2, pp. 17-24, March 1959.

Goldstein, A.J., Harmon, L.D. and Lesk, A.B. (1971), "Identification of Human Faces". Proc. IEEE, vol. 59, no. 5, pp. 748-760, May 1971.

Good, I.J. (1967), "The Loss of Information due to Clipping a Waveform". Information and Control, vol. 10, no.2, pp. 220-222, Feb. 1967.

Good, I.J. (1968), "A Five-Year Plan for Automatic Chess". In Dale and Michie 1968, pp. 89-118.

Greenblatt, R., Eastlake, D. and Crocker, S. (1967), "The Greenblatt Chess Program". 1967 Fass Joint Computer Conference, AFIPS Proc., vol. 31, Washington, D.C.: Thompson, 1967, pp. 801-810.

Grenander, U. (1969), "Foundations of Pattern Analysis". Quarterly of Applied Mathematics, vol. XXVII, no. 1, Section 1, April 1969.

Hájek, Jaroslav and Šidák, Zbyněk (1967), "Theory of Rank Tests". New York: Academic Press Inc., 1967.

Hald, A. (1962), "Statistical Theory with Engineering Applications". New York: John Wiley and Sons, Fifth Printing, 1962.

Harmon, L.D. (1972), "Automatic Recognition of Print and Script". Proc. IEEE, vol. 60, no. 10, pp. 1165-1176, Oct. 1972.

Harmon, L.D. and Lewis, E.R. (1966), "Neural Modeling". Physiological Rev., vol. 46, pp. 513-591, 1966.

Hellwarth, G.A. and Jones, G.D. (1968), "Automatic Conditioning of Speech Signals". IEEE Trans. on Audio and Electro-acoustics, vol. AU-16, no. 2, pp. 169-179, June 1968.

Highleyman, W.H. (1962a), "Design and Analysis of Pattern Recognition Experiments". Bell System Technical Journal, vol. 41, pp. 723-744, March 1962.

Highleyman, W.H. (1962b), "Linear Decision Functions, with Application to Pattern Recognition". Proc. IRE, vol. 50, no. 6, pp. 1501-1514, June 1962.

Ho, Y.-C. and Kashyap (1965), "An Algorithm for Linear Inequalities and its Applications". IEEE Trans. on Electr. Comp., vol. EC-14, no. 5, pp. 683-688, Oct. 1965.

Hodges, D.A. (1972), "Semiconductor Memories". New York: IEEE Press, 1972.

Horwitz, L.P. and Shelton, Jr., G.L. (1961), "Pattern Recognition Using Autocorrelation". Proc. IRE, vol. 49, no. 1, pp. 175-185, Jan. 1961.

Howard, R.A. (1967), "Value of Information Lotteries". IEEE Trans. on Systems, Science and Cybernetics, vol. SSC-3, no. 1, pp. 54-60, June 1967.

Hu, Ming-Kuei (1962), "Visual Pattern Recognition by Moment Invariants". IRE Trans. on Info. Theory, vol. IT-8, no. 2, pp. 179-187, Feb. 1962.

Ingram, M. and Preston, K. (1970), "Automatic Analysis of Blood Cells". Scientific American, pp. 72-82, Nov. 1970.

Irani, K.B. (1968), "A Finite-Memory Adaptive Pattern Recognizer". IEEE Trans. on Systems, Science and Cybernetics, vol. SSC-4, no. 1, pp. 2-11, March 1968.

Ito, T. (1968), "A Note on a General Expansion of Functions of Binary Variables". Information and Control, vol. 12, no. 3, pp. 206-211, March 1968.

Jaynes, E.T. (1968), "Prior Probabilities". IEEE Systems, Science and Cybernetics, vol. SSC-4, no. 3, pp. 227-241, Sep. 1968.

Kamentsky, L.A. and Liu, C.N. (1964), "A Theoretical and Experimental Study of a Model for Pattern Recognition". In Tou and Wilcox 1964, pp. 194-218.

Kanal, L.N. (1968), editor, "Pattern Recognition". Washington, D.C.: Thompson Book Comp., 1968.

Kashyap, R.L. and Blaydon, C.C. (1968), "Estimation of Probability Density and Distribution Functions". IEEE Trans. on Info. Theory, vol. IT-14, no. 4, pp. 549-556, July 1968.

Koford, I.S. and Groner, G.F. (1966), "The Use of an Adaptive Threshold Element to Design a Linear Optimal Classifier". IEEE Trans. on Info. Theory, vol. 12, no. 1, pp. 42-50, Jan. 1966.

Kullbach, S. (1969), "Information Theory and Statistics". New York: John Wiley and Sons, Inc., 1959.

Laski, Janusz (1968), "On the Probability Density Estimation". Proc. IEEE, vol. 56, no. 5, pp. 866-867, May 1968. (Letter).

Leary, R.W., Harlow, H.F., Settlage, P.H. and Greenwood, D.D. (1952), "Performance on Double-Alternation Problems by Normal and Brain-Injured Monkeys". Journal comp. physchol., vol. 45, pp. 576- 584, 1952.

Lehmann, E.L. (1959), "Testing Statistical Hypotheses". New York: John Wiley and Sons, Inc., 1959.

Lendaris, George G. and Stanley G.L. (1970), "Diffraction-Pattern Sampling for Automatic Pattern Recognition". Proc. IEEE, vol. 58, no. 2, pp. 198-216, Feb. 1970.

Levine, M.D. (1969), "Feature Extraction: A Survey". Proc. IEEE, vol. 57, no.8, pp. 1391-1407, Aug. 1969.

Lewis, P.M.,II (1962), "The Characteristic Selection Problem in Recognition Systems", IRE Trans. on Info. Theory, vol. IT-8, no. 2, pp. 171-179, Feb. 1962.

Lewis, P.M.,II and Coates, C.L. (1967), "Threshold Logic". New York: John Wiley and Sons, 1967.

Licklider, J.C.R. (1950), "Intelligibility of Amplitude-Dichotomized, Time-Quantized Speech Waves". Journal of the Acoustical Society of America, vol. 22, no. 6, pp. 820-823, Nov. 1950.

Lin, T.T. and Yau, S.S. (1967), "Bayesian Approach to the Optimization of Adaptive Systems". IEEE Trans. on Systems, Science and Cybernetics, vol. SSC-3, no. 2, pp. 77-85, Nov. 1967.

Lindgren, N. (1965), "Machine Recognition of Human Language, Part 3". IEEE Spectrum, vol. 2, no. 5, pp. 104-116, May 1965.

Liu, C.N. and Shelton, G.L., Jr. (1966), "An Experimental Investigation of a Mixed-Font Print Recognition System". IEEE Trans. on Electr. Comp., vol. EC-15, no. 4, pp. 916-925, Dec. 1966.

Ma, Y.-L. (1974), "The Pattern Recognition of Chinese Characters by Markov Chain Procedure". IEEE Trans. on Systems, Man, and Cybernetics, vol. SMC-4, no. 2, pp. 223-228, March 1974.

Marill, T. and Green, D.M. (1960), "Statistical Recognition Functions and the Design of Pattern Recognizers", IRE Trans. on Electr. Comp., vol. EC-9, no. 4, pp. 472-477, Dec. 1960.

Marill, T. and Green, D.M. (1963), "The Effectiveness of Receptors in Recognition Systems". IEEE Trans. on Info. Theory, vol. IT-9, no. 1, pp. 11-17, Jan. 1963.

Martin, Francis F. (1968), "Computer Modeling and Simulation". New York: John Wiley and Sons, Inc., 1968.

Masuda (1974), "Assesment of Handprinted Character Quality and its Applications to Machine Recognition". Paper in SIJCPR (1974).

Meisel, W.S. (1972), "Computer-oriented Approaches to Pattern Recognition". New York: Academic Press, 1972.

Mendel, J.M. and Fu, K.S. (1970), editors, "Adaptive, Learning and Pattern Recognition Systems. Theory and Applications". New York: Academic Press, 1970.

Michalsky, R.S. (1973), "AQVAL/1 - Computer Implementation of a Variable-Valued Logic System VL_1 and Examples of its Application to Pattern Recognition".   Paper in FIJCPR (1973).

Middleton, D. (1960), "An Introduction to Statistical Communication Theory". New York: McGraw-Hill, 1960.

Miller, G.A. and Frick, F.C. (1949), "Statistical Behavioristics and Sequences of Responses". Psychol. Revue, vol. 56, pp. 311-324, 1949.

Miller, R.G. (1961), "An Application of Multiple Discriminant
Analysis to the Probabilistic Prediction of Meteorological
Conditions Affecting Operational Decisions". Travelers'
Research Center, Inc., Hartford, Conn., TRC-M-4, March 1961.

Minsky, M. (1961), "Steps Toward Artificial Intelligence". Proc.
IRE, vol. 49, no. 1, pp. 8-30, Jan. 1961.

Minsky, M. (1963), "A Selected Descriptor-Indexed Bibliography to
the Literature on Artificial Intelligence". In Feigenbaum
and Feldman, 1963, pp. 453-523.

Minsky, M. and Papert, S. (1969), "Perceptrons". Cambridge, Mass.:
The MIT Press, 1969.

Muses, C.A. (1962), editor, "Aspects of the Theory of Artificial
Intelligence". New York: Plenum Press, 1962.

Nagy, G. (1968), "State of the ARt in Pattern Recognition". Proc.
IEEE, vol. 56, no. 5, pp. 836-862, May 1968.

Nagy, G. (1972), "Digital Image-Processing Activities in Remote
Sensing for Earth Resources". Proc. IEEE, vol. 60, no. 10,
pp. 1177-1200, Oct. 1972.

Nelson, G.D. and Levy, D.M. (1968), "A Dynamic Programming Approach
to the Selection of Pattern Features". IEEE Trans. on Systems,
Science and Cybernetics, vol. SSC-4, no. 2, July 1968.

Newell, A., Shaw, J.C. and Simon, H.A. (1963), "Chess-Playing Programs
and the Problem of Complexity". In Feigenbaum and Feldman,
1963, pp. 39-70.

Newell, A. and Simon, H.A. (1965), "An Example of Human Chess Play
in the Light of Chess Playing Programs". In "Progress in
Biocybernetics, vol. 2". Norbert Wiener and J.P. Schade,
editors, New York: American Elsevier Publishing Co., Inc., 1965.

Newman, E.B. and Gerstman, L.A. (1952), "A New Method for Analyzing
Printed English". Journal Exper. Psychol., vol. 44, pp. 114
-125, 1952.

Nilsson, N.J. (1965), "Learning Machines". New York: McGraw-Hill, 1965.

Niven, I. (1956), "Irrational Numbers". New York: John Wiley and Sons,
Inc., 1956. (Carus Math. Monograph no. 11).

Page, J. (1967), "Recognition of Patterns in Jet Engine Vibration
Signals". Digest of the First Annual IEEE Computer Conference
(Sep. 6-8, 1967), New York: IEEE Publications no. 16 C 51,
pp. 102-105.

Papoulis, A. (1965), "Probability, Random Variables, and Stochastic Processes". New York: McGraw-Hill, 1965.

Papoulis, A. (1966), "Error Analysis in Sampling Theory". Proc. IEEE, vol. 54, no. 7, pp. 947-955, July 1966.

Parmentier, R.D. (1970), "Neuristor Analysis Techniques for Nonlinear Distributed Electronic Systems". Proc. IEEE, vol. 58, no. 11, pp. 1829-1837, Nov. 1970.

Patrick, E.A., Stelmack, F.P. and Shen, L.Y.L. (1974), "Review of Pattern Recognition in Medical Diagnosis and Consulting Relative to a New System Model". IEEE Trans. on Systems, Man and Cybernetics, vol. SMC-4, no. 1, pp. 1-16, Jan. 1974.

Robbins, H. and Monro, S. (1951), "A Stochastic Approximation Method". Ann. Math. Stat., vol. 22, pp. 400-407, 1951.

Rosenblatt, F. (1962), "Principles of Neurodynamics". Washington, D.C.: Spartan, 1962.

Samuel, A.L. (1963), "Some Studies in Machine Learning Using the Game of Checkers". In Feigenbaum and Feldman, 1963, pp. 71-105.

Samuel, A.L. (1967), "Some Studies in Machine Learning Using the Game of Checkers, II. Recent Progress". IBM Journal of R and D, vol. 11, pp. 601-617, Nov. 1967.

Scarr, R.W.A. (1968), "Zero Crossings as a Means of Obtaining Spectral Information in Speech Analysis". IEEE Trans. on Audio and Electroacoustics, vol. AU-16, no. 2, pp. 247-255, June 1968.

Sebestyen, G.S. (1962), "Decision-Making Processes in Pattern Recognition". New York: The Macmillan Company, 1962.

Sebestyen, G. and Edie, J. (1966), "An Algorithm for Non-Parametric Pattern Recognition". IEEE Trans. on Electr. Comp., vol. EC-15, no. 6, pp. 908-915, Dec. 1966.

Selfridge, O.G. (1959), "Pandemonium: A Paradigm for Learning". In Mechanization of Thought Processes", London: Her Majesty's Stationary Office, 1959, pp. 513-526; reprinted in Uhr 1966, pp. 339-348.

Selin, I. (1965), "Detection Theory". Princeton, New Jersey: Princeton University Press, 1965.

Siegel, S. (1956), "Non-Parametric Statistics for the Behavioral Sciences". New York: McGraw-Hill, 1956.

SIJCPR (1974), "The Proceedings of the Second International Joint Conference on Pattern Recognition". Copenhagen, 1974. IEEE Catalog no. 74CHO 885-4C.

SIJCPR (1974), "BM". The papers from the sessions on "Bio-Medical Applications" in FIJCPR (1973) and SIJCPR (1974) are representative of the state of the art.

Solomonoff, R.I. (1966), "Some Recent Work in Artificial Intelligence". Proc. IEEE, vol. 54. no. 12, pp. 1687-1697, Dec. 1966.

Specht, D.F. (1967), "Generation of Polynominal Discriminant Functions for Pattern Recognition". IEEE Trans. on Electr. Comp., vol. EC-16, no. 3, pp. 308-319, June 1967.

Spragins, J. (1965), "A Note on the Iterative Application of Bayes' Rule". IEEE Trans. on Info. Theory, vol. IT-11, no. 1, pp. 544-549, Oct. 1965.

Steinbuch, K. and Widrow, B. (1966), "A Critical Comparison of Two Kinds of Adaptive Networks". IEEE Trans. on Electr. Comp., vol. EC-14, no. 5, pp. 737-740, Oct. 1966.

Strakhov, N.A. and Kurz, L. (1968), "An Upper Bound on the Zero-Crossing Distribution". Bell System Technical Journal, vol. 47, n0. 4, pp. 529-547, April 1968.

Strand, R.C. (1972), "Optical-Image Recognition for Experiments in the Track Chambers of High-Energy Physics". Proc. IEEE, vol. 62, no. 10, pp. 1122-1137, Oct. 1972.

Sugiura, T. and Higashiuwatoko, T. (1968), "A Method for the Recognition of Japanese Hiragana Characters". IEEE Trans. on Info. Theory, vol. IT-14, no. 2, pp. 226-233, March 1968.

Tamura, S., Higuchi, S. and Tanaka, K. (1971), "Pattern Classification Based on Fuzzy Relations". IEEE Trans. on Systems, Man and Cybernetics, vol. SMC-1, no. 1, pp. 61-66, Jan. 1971.

Thomas, R.B. and Kassler, M. (1967), "Character Recognition in Context". Information and Control, vol. 10, no. 1, pp. 43-64, Jan. 1967.

Tomiyasu, K. (1974), "Remote Sensing of the Earth by Microwaves". Proc. IEEE, vol. 62, no. 1, pp. 86-92, Jan. 1974.

Tooley, J.R. (1962), "Thresholding and Microminiaturization with Semi-Conductors". In Foerster, H.V., and Zopf, G.W., editors, "Principles of Self-Organization", pp. 511-520, New York: Pergamon Press, 1962.

Tou, J.T. (1967), editor, "Computer and Information Sciences - II". New York: Academic Press, 1967.

Tou, J.T. and Wilcox, R.H. (1964), editors, "Computer and Information Sciences". Washington, D.C.: Spartan Books, Inc., 1964.

Uhr, L. and Vossler, C. (1961), "A Pattern-Recognition Program that Generates, Evaluates, and Adjusts Its Own Operators". 1961 Proceedings of the Western Joint Computer Conference, pp. 555-569; reprinted in Feigenbaum and Feldman, 1963, pp. 251-268; again reprinted in Uhr, 1966, pp. 349-364.

Uhr, L. (1965), "Pattern Recognition" in "Electronic Information Handling", A. Kent and O.E. Taulbee, editors, Washington, D.C.: Spartan Books, Inc., 1965, pp. 51-72; reprinted in Uhr, 1966, pp. 365-381.

Uhr, L. (1966), editor, "Pattern Recognition". New York: John Wiley and Sons, Inc., 1966.

Wagner, T.G. (1968), "The Rate of Convergence of an Algorithm for Recovering Functions from Noisy Measurements Taken at Randomly Selected Points". IEEE Trans. on Systems, Science and Cybernetics, vol. SSC-4, no. 2, July 1968.

Watanabe, S. (1972), editor, "Frontiers of Pattern Recognition". New York: Academic Press, 1972.

Wee, W.G. and Fu, K.S. (1968), "An Adaptive Procedure for Multiclass Pattern Classification". IEEE Trans. on Comp., vol. C-17, no. 2, pp. 178-182, Feb. 1968.

Widrow, B., Groner, G.F., Hu, M.I.C., Smith, F.W., Specht, D.F. and Talbert, L.R. (1963), "Practical Applications for Adaptive Data-Processing Systems". WESCON 1963, paper no. 11.4.

Wilks, S.S. (1962), "Mathematical Statistics". New York: John Wiley and Sons, Inc., 1962.

Winder, R.O. (1963), "Threshold Logic in Artificial Intelligence". In the book "Artificial Intelligence", Publication no. S-142 pp. 107-138, published by IEEE, Box A, Lenox Hill Station, New York, N.Y., 1963.

Yau, S.S. and Yang, C.C. (1966), "Pattern Recognition by Using an Associative Memory". IEEE Trans. on Electr. Comp., vol. EC-15 no. 6, pp. 941-944, Dec. 1966. (Short note).

Yau, S.S. and Ling, T.T. (1968), "On the Upper Bound of the Probability of Error of a Linear Pattern Classifier for Probabilistic Pattern Classes". Proc. IEEE, vol. 56, no. 3, pp. 321-322, March 1968. (Letter).

Yau, S.S. and Schumpert, S.M. (1968), "Design of Pattern Classifiers with Updating Property Using Stochastic Approximation Technique". IEEE Trans. on Comp., vol. C-17, no. 9, Sep. 1968.

Young, T.Y. and Huggins, W.H. (1964), "Computer Analysis of Electro-Cardiograms Using a Linear Regression Technique". IEEE Trans. on Bio-Medical Engineering, vol. BME-11, pp. 60-67, July 1964.

Druck: Novographic, Ing. Wolfgang Schmid, A-1230 Wien.